THE JUDAS SYNDROME

Why Good People Do Awful Things

GEORGE K. SIMON JR., PH.D.

Abingdon Press
Nashville

THE JUDAS SYNDROME
WHY GOOD PEOPLE DO AWFUL THINGS

Copyright © 2013 by Abingdon Press

All rights reserved.

No part of this work may be reproduced or transmitted in any form or by any means, electronic or me-chanical, including photocopying and recording, or by any information storage or retrieval system, except as may be expressly permitted by the 1976 Copyright Act or in writing from the publisher. Requests for permission can be addressed to Permissions, The United Methodist Publishing House, P.O. Box 801, 201 Eighth Avenue South, Nashville, TN 37202-0801, or e-mailed to permissions@umpublishing.org.

The vignettes in this book are for illustration only.
Any similarity to real persons or actual events is purely coincidental.

This book is printed on acid-free paper.

Library of Congress Cataloging-in-Publication Data has been requested.

ISBN 978-1-4267-5109-7

Scripture quotations are taken from the New Revised Standard Version of the Bible, copyright 1989, Division of Christian Education of the National Council of the Churches of Christ in the United States of America. Used by permission. All rights reserved.

13 14 15 16 17 18 19 20 21 22—10 9 8 7 6 5 4 3 2 1

MANUFACTURED IN THE UNITED STATES OF AMERICA

CONTENTS

ACKNOWLEDGMENTS

I owe a supreme debt of gratitude to my editor, Kathy Armistead, for providing me the opportunity to write the kind of book I've long wanted to write and for making the suggestions necessary to make the manuscript more readable.

There is no way to adequately convey the debt I owe my wife, Sherry. I cherish her as my toughest critic as well as my strongest and most unwavering source of support. But even more than that, the level of her commitment to our marriage as a vehicle to grow not only in the love for each other but also in the love of our God has been for me both awe-inspiring and humbling.

I thank God daily for the family I always dreamed of having but once feared was impossible to secure. My sons, daughter-in-law, and grandchildren are but a few of the countless blessings I enjoy but know sincerely I have never merited.

Last, I am grateful for the opportunity to have worked with so many individuals over the years who taught me so much, enriched my life, and helped me appreciate the power of honesty and faith. It is to all of them that I dedicate this book.

INTRODUCTION

Judas betrayed with a kiss. Even people who we think are our friends can disavow and betray us. Are they simply bad people or are they basically decent folks whose weakness of faith and deficiencies of character became exposed when put to the test? If the latter is true, there's a little Judas in all of us.

One of the most sobering and unavoidable realities of life is that bad things sometimes happen. Because we are naturally troubled by such circumstances, religious sages and other observers of the human condition have struggled over the years to explain why these painful events occur in our lives. Some psychologists tell us that darkness lurks deep within each of us, but they cannot fully explain why some people prefer the dark and resist the light.

Consider the Milgram experiment. Imagine you are participating in a study. Like all the participants, you freely signed up. After you listen to the thorough instructions, the leader pairs you up with another participant. He then asks you to give your partner what you believe to be an increasingly high-voltage shock from a generator if he or she fails to answer correctly. Would you be one of the sixty-five percent who *followed* instructions and gave his or her partner an almost fatal dose of electricity for failing to respond as directed?

Or consider the well-known bystander effect. A young woman is assaulted on a pool table while a crowd of onlookers do nothing. Despite the fact that there is ample opportunity, no one calls for help or intervenes. In fact, according to psychological research, the greater number of bystanders, the less likely it is that any of them will help.

Yes, bad things happen, and often good people are the cause.

It used to be, in ancient times, that people believed bad things—including natural disasters such as earthquakes and volcanic eruptions—happened because various gods were not sufficiently appeased by the sacrifices that people offered them. And even during the time of Jesus, many Jews believed that people suffered misfortune of all sorts, including physical illnesses, because they or someone in their families had incurred the wrath of God. Those who prospered, they reasoned, must be living righteously, meriting God's favor, whereas those who were suffering must be impure and only experiencing the just deserts of their impiety. But no matter the time or place, human beings are innately driven to seek meaning and understanding, especially when things don't go their way. And because suffering is such a significant yet undesirable part of our lives, we continually try to come up with acceptable explanations for why bad things happen to us.

This book is not intended to be a comprehensive look at human suffering or an exploration of all the possible reasons bad things happen. Bad things occur for lots of reasons, sometimes perhaps because God permits them. The world in which we live is a wondrous product of creation. But it is definitely not heaven, and we are less than perfect. Our world and our lives are prone to unpredictable and sometimes unpreventable calamities. And contrary to what many believe, many things occur purely coincidentally or accidentally. They are no one's fault. Experiencing both the good and the bad just seems to be part of living in this world. But the inevitability of having bad things happen, or even good people doing bad things, does not mean that we are left helpless with no recourse.

This book is about common and preventable ways bad things happen in our lives and the role that faith—more specifically, genuine faith in Christ—can play in avoiding them or dealing with the pain that happens as a result. What is really important to know is that because much of what we suffer stems from our own shortcomings, missteps, and character deficiencies, placing our trust in Christ and his message of love, righteousness, forgiveness, and especially spiritual rebirth, provides the gateway to a rich, abundant, and joyful life—the life that God intends for us. And although this book is written primarily for a Christian audience, I hope that the major issues it addresses resonate for followers of any belief system, especially those who have taken to heart their faith community's most tested, validated, and enduring tenets for living a fulfilled, responsible, and principle-driven life.

Suffering of one type or another seems an all too familiar aspect of life. In this imperfect world, we simply can't avoid pain and anguish. And suffering can serve a truly redemptive role in the purification of our souls. Still, it takes considerable faith to find the value in it, especially when, from our perspective, it appears senseless or needless. The larger problem for us and the subject of this book is the suffering that results when people make unloving choices.

There's a big difference between the bad things that simply

happen and the bad or evil things that occur as the result of the things people sometimes do, and this book focuses on the pain brought about by human action. Face it, we are all unloving sometimes. All of us do good and bad things, because we are creatures with free will. Even the best of us "fall short of the glory of God" (Romans 3:23). But that does not mean that the proliferation of evil is inevitable. Evil survives through human choice. And although it's extremely difficult, we do have the power to avoid or even stop it. Our God treasures us with steadfast loving-kindness; only a cruel and sadistic god would throw us into a world where he would command us to be good and seek his council and then rob us of the ability to make it happen. We have the power to choose healing over injury, generosity over covetousness, compassion over indifference. But the ways of the world are a subtle yet forceful teacher, and they tempt us to act in unloving ways. That's why faith is so crucial to our spiritual well-being. It takes considerable faith to approach and live life on terms quite different from those we often see around us.

How evil comes into our lives is a matter of debate and has been from biblical times. Jesus spoke to this very issue when he and his disciples were chided by some religious leaders and legal scholars for eating with dirty hands, thus allowing the "impurities" of the world to "defile" them. It was not uncommon at the time for pious Jews to believe that, in order to keep themselves pure in spirit, they had to exercise great caution about what kind of earthly impurities they came in contact with. And while there's little doubt that impurities of one type or another can adversely affect us, Jesus emphasized (in Matthew 15 and Mark 7) that "nothing outside" (Mark 7:15) that enters us has the power to defile us spiritually. Rather what makes us dirty or impure are the ill intentions in our hearts that emanate from us (such as envy, lewdness, deceit, slander).

A predominant message throughout Christ's earthly ministry is that while all sorts of unseemly things might occur in our lives, it's our *response* that matters most. Our sojourn on earth is designed not so much for our personal pleasure or freedom from discomfort as it is for our spiritual development and fulfillment, which can involve substantial pain at times. And people of faith recognize that in order to prevent many of the bad things that plague our lives, we need to pay less attention to the unseemly things that might come our way and be more mindful of the condition of our own hearts from which real evil arises.

The primary purpose of this book is to illustrate the evils that arise out of spiritual ill health, to call attention to the kinds of bad things that happen when otherwise good people behave in problematic ways, and to reaffirm the reality of faith in Christ and his message as the essential means by which we can be saved from ourselves—our ignoble natures. Such faith, then, can deliver us from evil and renew us to live productive, meaningful lives.

For the most part, bad things happen when:

1. bad people do bad things. Now, I'm well aware that some might object to my use of the term "bad people." All of my training in psychology (and even the tenets of my faith) admonished me never to condemn the person per se but rather to condemn the harmful behavior he or she might display (that is, hate the sin but not the sinner). And although that axiom is rooted in a great truth, it's extremely important to recognize there are individuals in this world with very serious defects

of character. These are not the relatively well-adjusted or "good" individuals who occasionally do bad things, but those who have fashioned for themselves a personality (that is, a preferred way of perceiving the world, thinking about things, and relating to others) that predisposes them to frequently and deliberately do things to exploit, hurt, or abuse others. Some of these folks can appear quite benign or even "good" on the surface because of their capacity to make favorable impressions. But the very nature of their character defects casts a dark shadow upon their souls, keeps them at odds with the faith that could heal them, and regularly brings evil not only into their own lives but also into the lives of those who might come into contact with them. It's the way they are (and in some cases, the way they ardently *prefer* to be) that inevitably leads to the bad things they do and the harm they cause others. So, although it's arguably not completely appropriate to use the label, it's also not totally inaccurate to use the term "bad" to describe such individuals.

2. otherwise decent people (that is, folks with common, minor flaws but without *serious* character defects) are put to the test by adversity or temptation. Sometimes, their internal controls or level of commitment to their ideals are not solid enough to hold up under times of duress. Other times, their insufficient or shallow faith allows them to be too easily undermined by their shortcomings and weaknesses. This can apply to even those who see themselves as "saved" because they have openly acknowledged their acceptance of Christ. The problem

comes when their faith in the Lord and in his eternal living Word is not rooted deeply enough. So when difficult times or attractive temptations come, they have insufficient resources to keep them from doing harm.

3. basically good people do things, sometimes even with good intentions but nonetheless in significant ignorance, leading to bad results. There's profound truth in the saying "the road to hell is paved with good intentions." It's often not enough to merely mean well. And sometimes, an act that appears motivated by a sincere and benevolent desire is really the manifestation of a person's fear, clouded judgment, or deficient faith. It's an unfortunate fact (one that helping professionals often have to deal with) that basically good people, with sincerity of heart and purpose, often make choices that inadvertently "enable" bad things to happen.

4. basically good people don't do enough to prevent bad things (that is, commit "sins of omission" through apathy, neglect, fear, indifference). It's one thing to say you believe. It's another thing to affirm and manifest that faith through fervent, virtuous action. Many of us lack sufficient conviction in our espoused beliefs to be actively propelled into righteous behavior. And as the old adage often attributed (though many think incorrectly) to Edmund Burke warns: "the only thing necessary for the triumph of evil is that good men do nothing."

As a practicing therapist for many years, I have witnessed first-hand the evil that enters the lives of people who fail to face and reckon with their deficiencies of character and who lack or lose hold of the faith that might have saved them. But challenging and encouraging these individuals to find or reclaim their faith and to honestly and persistently address their shortcomings is a most rewarding enterprise. I have been blessed to observe the power a sincere change of heart can have in transforming a person's life. In fact, without it, no real change can actually occur. So it is with confidence that I assert that *faith*—more specifically, genuine faith in Christ—*saves*. I'm not speaking here of merely accepting the notion that Christ's willing death was a perfect sacrifice that atoned for the sinfulness of the human race and opened the gates of paradise. I'm also not talking about the willingness to simply verbally assert one's acceptance of Christ as personal Savior. Rather, I'm saying that really *knowing* Christ—who he really is, what his mission is all about, the power of the example he came to give, what he reveals to us about our nature and the nature of God, the substance of what he commands his followers to *do*—and then putting our complete faith and trust in him and responding with Christ-like, grace-filled service has the ability to utterly and completely transform and elevate a person's life.

What I have witnessed during my years as a therapist is that most of the time, bad things occur in people's lives when faith is absent or lacking and our baser instincts prevail. That's why faith in Christ and his living, eternal, and transforming word is so fundamental to health and well-being. Still, believing in who Christ is, the meaning of all that he taught us, and the importance of what he commands us to do is both difficult and contrary to many human instincts. But for those who take the leap of faith *in him* (and, without a doubt, it is one heck of a leap!), an entirely new existence is waiting. That's because he is—just as he claimed to be—the very substance or "bread" of real, abundant, and everlasting life. If we really want to live, we must literally let our world-fashioned selves go and be remade in him. We must believe in him to the point that we are willing to stop feeding ourselves on the attractive but poisonous offerings of this material world and consume *him*—to make him an integral part of who we are and what we do on a daily basis. We do more than incorporate him into our reality temporarily. Rather, we grant him permanent residence in the deepest recesses of our hearts and souls. Then, as Paul proclaims, he is in us and lives through us. We cease to be who we were and are made new. This is the real Christian faith— a faith not easily undertaken and one that cannot be sustained alone. And make no mistake, such faith truly *saves*.

Believing in who Christ really is and surrendering oneself to him was a challenge even for some of his closest disciples. Judas had his own ideas about what the promised messiah would be like, and he was not alone in coming to the conclusion that Jesus did not fit the bill. Moreover, he, like others, saw Jesus as a potential threat to a very different kind of movement—a movement to which he was fervently committed. He might have once believed in the Lord, but his deeper convictions became evident when he sold him out for thirty pieces of silver and marked him for delivery into his enemies' hands with a kiss.

So, when you examine things more deeply, it becomes apparent that it was not just Jesus that Judas betrayed with his actions. With that fateful kiss, Judas also betrayed himself, the condition of his heart, and the true character of his own flawed faith. Despite his frequent, intimate contact with the Lord, Judas could not come to believe Jesus was the answer to his own or his people's needs. It appears he at least regarded Christ as a gifted teacher, as evidenced by his betrayal greeting of "Rabbi." And the fact that he later regretted his actions suggests he thought Jesus a righteous man who did not deserve to suffer the humiliating death that would result. But he did not believe Jesus to be the promised one, and Judas's kiss betrayed his erroneous but more deeply held convictions.

It is worth saying again: there's a little Judas in all of us. Even Christians cause some pretty awful things to happen, sometimes inadvertently, sometimes by not doing enough, and sometimes even on purpose, and with malice. And while we might publicly confess Christ as God incarnate imparting to us the very words of eternal life, we often behave in a manner that suggests we really believe him merely a good and decent man with some noble but impractical advice for conducting our lives. Our actions betray our hearts and the true character of our faith.

Even the most ardent believers can succumb to the "Judas Syndrome." The faith that can really save us is not easily embraced on a daily basis or sustained alone. We need the inspiration and support of a community of believers who, despite their own failed tests of character, continue to trust in Christ's message of love, repentance, and forgiveness. This book is meant to provide such inspiration and support by sharing the stories of several persons whose faith and character were put to the test. Their stories attest to how faith in Christ provides the gateway to the rich and abundant life God intends for all of us.

Caveat

The vignettes presented in this book are fictionalized accounts of actual events and circumstances known to the author as the result of direct access to actual case files or information provided to the author from reliable sources. In some cases, elements of different situations have been combined to prevent the discernment of any particular individual or circumstance. In all cases the names, professions, locations, situations, and other biographical data have been altered to preserve anonymity and privacy to the greatest degree possible. Great care was also taken to ensure that any alterations of details did not distort or inaccurately portray the fundamental psychological, emotional, and spiritual realities and principles the stories are intended to illustrate.

Although the author and publisher have made every effort to ensure the accuracy and completeness of information provided in this book, they assume no responsibility for errors, inaccuracies, omissions, or any inconsistencies herein. Any slights of people, places, or organizations are unintentional.

CHAPTER 1

WHEN BAD PEOPLE DO BAD THINGS

B ad things happen and good people are often the cause, but not always. Before we look at why good people do bad things, we need to separate the sheep from the goats and consider that sometimes bad things happen because, as much as we might like to think otherwise, there are bad people. As hard as it is for many of us to accept, there are individuals whose character is so deeply flawed that it predisposes them to do bad things much of the time (Simon, *Character Disturbance*, 34–36). They might have been born with troubling inclinations or shaped by life full of tragedy. But whatever the cause and even if their first impression is favorable, bad people do exist. In fact, it's precisely because this is such a hard thing to accept that many folks become entrapped in and remain in toxic relationships (Simon, *In Sheep's Clothing*, 140).

When I speak of "bad people," I'm not referring to folks who are generally well-adjusted, God-fearing, and well-meaning

1

but nonetheless injure others in a moment of personal weakness and with some degree of obliviousness. Rather, I'm speaking of those individuals who know well the difference between right and wrong and understand what most others might regard as appropriate and responsible conduct, but who knowingly and purposely adopt an approach to life and dealing with others that is adverse, inconsiderate, and reckless. Such individuals frequently, and often deliberately, bring pain into the lives of those with whom they come into contact.

Basically good folks have their shortcomings to be sure; they can also do things that hurt others. And this is not to say that bad people can't sometimes do good things. But because they harbor unresolved emotional wounds, conflicts, and so forth, about which they are often not even consciously aware, much of the time when basically decent people do bad things, they truly don't know what they're doing or even why they're really doing it when they cause harm. Not only do they lack malevolent intent, they also most often regret and feel appropriate guilt about the harm they might have caused once they realize the nature of what they've done.

But there are some folks who knowingly, intentionally, and repeatedly do things that hurt others. Chief among these individuals are the narcissistic or *egotistic* personalities, who pursue their own selfish desires with pathological indifference to the rights and concerns of others, and the *aggressive* personalities, who get what they want by deliberately trampling the rights and concerns of others (Simon, *Character Disturbance*, 98). The vignettes in this chapter are intended to highlight how these seriously character-deficient individuals wreak havoc upon the lives of those around them, and how the absence of faith in anything greater than themselves keeps them from becoming better persons.

When There's No Room in One's Heart for God

For God to dwell in us, we must first make a space for him. But some people simply have no space in their hearts for a power greater than themselves. Oh, they might outwardly profess a belief in God. Sometimes, they will even "protest" some kind of religious conviction to the point of near absurdity. But in the deepest recesses of their souls, they can barely even *conceive* of a power greater than themselves, let alone *turn themselves over* to one. The very idea of humbling and subordinating themselves—in complete faith and trust—to the unseen, incomprehensible, great "I AM" is anathema to them. The various gods these folks truly worship and their lack of faith in the one true source of life most often come to light when circumstances put their characters ardently to the test.

Chief among the gods that egotistic or narcissistic characters worship is the grandiose image they have of themselves (Simon, *Character Disturbance*, 91). They regard themselves as inordinately "special" and view nearly everyone else as pathetically inferior. They're often so convinced of their special status that they feel entitled to do whatever they please in their dealings with those they perceive are beneath them. And because they have no concept of anything more powerful or important than they are, there's nothing in their mental or psychological framework to inhibit them from selfishly using and abusing those around them.

I've counseled many times the kind of person depicted in the vignette that follows. They've worn different faces, have come from different backgrounds, and were of various colors and races. Yet they were remarkably the same with respect to the essential features of their character. Many were quite accomplished and successful, at least by worldly standards. But their character defects generally rendered them failures in their relationships. Their stories were often so similar that it wasn't difficult to fashion an illustrative example.

The Story of Philip and Nan

Philip would be the first to tell you that he knew himself pretty well. He was also not ashamed to admit how much he liked the person he was. From the outset, he made it clear that he agreed to make an appointment with a therapist mostly because his wife, Nan, was pressuring him to do so. She had threatened to file for divorce unless he got some help. He didn't really see the need for it, he complained, and he readily admitted he had always been more than a little leery of "head shrinks." But he'd promised Nan he would see someone, and he was also a little bit curious about what a professional might say about his situation.

After introducing myself to Philip, I informed him that I would most likely defer a final decision about working with him until we had visited a few times and I had a chance to complete both an evaluation of his circumstances and an assessment of his "appropriateness" for the kind of character development enterprise in which I typically engage. He appeared somewhat incredulous about this and more than a bit fascinated. Still, he assented to the conditions.

Philip would be considered a remarkable success in life by any number of commonly accepted standards. Coming from relatively humble beginnings, he was able to land a job with a large corporation and steadily rose through the ranks of the company, eventually making it all the way to the top. He had accumulated substantial monetary wealth, social prestige, personal power, and political influence. He knew a lot of important people and wielded a lot of influence. The world, it seemed, was his oyster.

Philip had done some very good things in his life. Under his leadership, his company regularly donated substantial sums (not incidentally enjoying noteworthy publicity and significant tax breaks in the process) to several popular and worthy causes. But Philip had also done many bad things, some of which were even illegal. Most of the time, he was able to elude detection, and even when he did get caught, he had the intellectual, legal, and financial resources to get himself out of trouble. Philip never fretted. He generally did just as he pleased without fear of sanction. He never experienced a moment's hesitation, even when contemplating what many might view as unthinkable. That's because Philip did all the bad things he'd ever done for the very same reason he did almost everything else in his life: he felt he *could* and *should* be able to do them.

To anyone who inquired, Philip would insist that he believed in God, and would readily point to his hefty donations not only to his church but also to various charitable causes as indications of his commitment to leading a "Christian life." But as would eventually become all too apparent, in truth Philip recognized no entity or power greater than himself. This made anything but self-worship virtually impossible. And even when Philip gave, he appeared mainly concerned for the recognition that would be afforded him or his company as benefactor. In the deepest recesses of his soul, there was only one entity Philip ever really believed in, worshiped, or served: himself.

More than anything else, Philip relished the notion that he was a self-made man, and he was happy to boast that fact to anyone he met. He happily attributed his successes in life to his tenacity and hard work. Nobody ever gave him anything, he asserted with fervor. And he would readily admit that he might not have the talent or intelligence of some of his friends, acquaintances, and colleagues. But he believed in himself because he had determination and the moxie to make the best of any challenging circumstance. By his own account, he was shrewd, confident, and always a force with which to contend. And he was undeniably and unabashedly proud of those facts. Place before him any challenge, he would boast, and he had confidence he would emerge a winner.

At the moment, however, Philip was in a most unusual and difficult place. Nan had recently come across evidence that he had been having affairs for years, had been engaging in some accounting irregularities into which the government was now looking, and had quietly been pilfering their accounts to the point that the family's once substantial savings were now virtually nonexistent. She suddenly found herself seeing what once appeared as an almost idyllic world crumbling all around her. And she'd had enough of what she now knew to be his lengthy history of lies and deceit and was seriously contemplating divorce.

I wish I could say that Philip showed signs of concern over the possibility he might lose the woman he purportedly loved and cherished, or that he was experiencing some degree of distress because of the pain he had caused her. But as the evaluation progressed, it became quite apparent that he was far more concerned about the potential personal costs (in money, property, and image) he could incur as the result of a divorce. Some other things also became clear: Philip had been using some clever tactics to prey on Nan's conscientious nature in the hopes that she would be manipulated into standing by him. He frequently and openly lamented to her that she would be deserting him just when he anticipated some very difficult times ahead and really needed her support. And he questioned the sincerity of her religious convictions in view of the fact that she was considering renouncing her marriage vows. He also argued that she really owed it to him to help preserve their home, lifestyle, family, and reputation he'd worked so hard to maintain. And when these arguments did not appear to be enough, he took aim at Nan's sensibilities. He pointed to the fact that when she told him she wanted him to get some help, despite the many reservations he had about it, he honored his promise to do whatever it took to keep things from falling apart. So, he asserted, it was only fair for her to hold off seeking a divorce as long as he was agreeing to see a therapist. But Philip's behavior made it clear that it was for largely practical and selfish reasons, and *not* because he felt horribly about having done wrong, had deeply hurt the woman who had been faithful to him for years, and was internally troubled and motivated to make some crucial changes in himself to avoid inflicting pain on loved ones again, that he had come to a therapist's office.

It never sat all that well with Philip that I would reserve judgment about whether I would even accept him as a client until I had completed an assessment of his suitability. For one thing, he'd never heard of a situation in which someone who supposedly made his or her living talking to people willing to pay good money to have someone else listen to them and help them deal with their problems would actually consider turning the opportunity down. But inasmuch as trust is the very foundation of any potentially therapeutic relationship, it was important for me to acknowledge that I wasn't sure things would work out—at least at this particular moment in time and in view of the kind of work I had in mind. Still, by the end of the second visit, Philip was already putting some pressure on me to commit. "You'd have to agree, wouldn't you, George, that it's a bit unusual for a person who is supposed to be in the business of helping people, to actually consider turning away someone who's come to them for help? Besides, you don't really know me, anyway. Shouldn't you be giving me a chance?" Part of me wanted to retort that I'd spent the better part of our first two sessions making structured clinical observations and gathering relevant background information. Another part was tempted to point out that we'd spent several hours outside of sessions gathering history and incorporating Nan's input, and that the evaluation was not yet over. I also thought about calling attention to some of the tactics I felt he was using to subtly coerce me into giving him what he wanted, such as leveling (putting the authority figure on the same level as the person needing guidance), posturing (trying to put the other person on the defensive), and subtle guilt-tripping and shaming (insinuating that there was something not only wrong but also shameful and possibly even unethical about a professional "helper" actually considering not providing services to a supposedly needy and willing client) (Simon, *Character Disturbance*, 188–93). I was also more than tempted to point out that Philip had already spoken at length about what was mostly motivating him to come and see me in the first place, as well as what he clearly announced that he wasn't too interested in pursuing. But rather than address those issues just yet, I simply and cordially reaffirmed that I would discuss my overall assessment at the end of our last evaluative session. I could tell he was provoking a defensive reaction from me and I observed that, sadly, I too had some narcissistic tendencies that I needed to address but, obviously, not with my client.

During our visits, there were many ways Philip tried to put and keep me on the defensive, which is a cardinal sign of a serious character disturbance in which a person too readily, too often, and too intensely tries to assume the more dominant and controlling position in a relationship. He also immediately and consistently addressed me by my first name and made subtly derogatory comments about the field of psychology and the various mental health professions, which I regarded as a possible sign of a character intent on either establishing a position of superiority or diminishing another's position, especially one who would naturally otherwise occupy a position of relative authority. But it was not until I asked him to give me some details about the accounting irregularities at work that had gotten him into trouble that Philip revealed the most significant features of his character fairly clearly. "Boy, could I write a book about the useless waste of time and money in our government and how absolutely stupid the idiots at the IRS can be," he ranted. "And to think our tax dollars pay the salaries of these dummies," he added. Then he told me how common it was for folks in his line of work who had access to certain cash accounts to temporarily "borrow" funds as a sort of informal loan with every intention of paying back the money when circumstances permitted. So, he asserted, taking the money wasn't really that big of an issue. Besides, it was because of *his* hard work and acumen that the money was even there in the first place! His real mistakes, which he boasted that he was "perfectly willing to admit," were that he'd lost track of how much he'd borrowed and was "stupid" to have been so sloppy in the manner in which he'd handled the transactions. His sloppiness led to some questions about his tax returns and got the IRS looking into things. He should have been much more discreet, that's all. Philip never addressed the decisions he made or the actions he took that got him into trouble. Nor did he address the rightness or wrongness of those decisions. Doing so would have provided a prime opportunity for him to express genuine responsibility and possibly even some regret for his behavior. But over the entire course of the evaluation, all he offered me was a series of justifications for seriously improper acts, a trivialization of the nature of his transgressions, and weak, token admissions of minor errors in practical judgment.

Things began to add up pretty quickly. Philip's sense of entitlement was massive, and any degree of conscience he might have was markedly impaired. He was displaying some of the most telltale features of individuals with a particular kind of character disturbance. And as the rest of his history came to light, it was clear that his sense of entitlement had been with him a long time, reflected in many subtle ways long before his current problems surfaced. When he threw lavish parties at his home, he didn't ask his neighbors if they minded folks parking in front of their homes or blocking their driveways. He simply took for granted that they should understand. And if they didn't, he dismissed them as hapless, jealous souls whose discontent was probably rooted in their envy that so many notables in town were always gathering at his house instead of theirs. And when he discovered his wife kept a diary, he didn't have to justify reading it without asking her permission. After all, a wife shouldn't keep any secrets from her husband, anyway. Now as to why he never told her about the affairs he had—at least the three he distinctly remembered and that really counted—that was simple: she'd probably only get the wrong impression of him. A man who travels can get awfully lonesome at times. And the hotel rooms in the cities he had to regularly visit could feel so terribly empty. Besides, the women with whom he kept company were merely dinner dates and sexual companions, not real lovers. They really meant nothing. So you could say he was never truly unfaithful because Nan was the only one he really cared about. You could even say he never reneged on the spirit of his marriage vows. He might have had multiple liaisons, but he wasn't really being unfaithful. He was still a great guy, worthy of Nan's love and devotion. Listening to Philip, one could even be tempted to think he had every right to do all the things for which he was now in trouble.

By the end of the evaluation period, the most troubling aspect of Philip's character would become abundantly clear: he thought far too much of himself. In psychological terms, this means he had a substantially bloated ego and an exaggerated sense of self-importance. His narcissism was of such a quality and degree that it was truly pathological. Traditionally, the manifestation of inflated self-esteem has been thought to be due to an underlying insecurity and impoverished sense of self, anxiously compensated for with a pretentious but false self-presentation. And while this kind of psychological dynamic can sometimes be accurate, it's not always true (Simon, *Character Disturbance*, 49–51). And in Philip's case, the grandiose self-appraisal he displayed was much less a compensation for insecurity and much more a reflection of his sincere, if unwarranted conviction about his special status among others. And it was his ardent belief in this special status that cultivated in him such a remarkable sense of entitlement. It's why he never felt any compunction about doing whatever he wished to do, regardless of how others might regard his actions.

Philip talked often about the successes he had achieved in life. He appeared especially proud to explain just how he got to be where he is. He spent much of the second and part of the third visit extolling his unwavering determination and commitment to hard work. That was the reason for his success, he asserted. And while there could be no doubt about the role hard work played, certain other acknowledgments were conspicuous by their absence. Philip never spoke about the ample gifts and talents he been granted by nature, the many fortunate opportunities afforded him, or the fortuitousness of circumstance. He never acknowledged the sacrifices of his parents, the devotion and support of his wife, the role of his teachers, the blessings of freedom in the country in which he was fortunate to have been born, and so forth. In short, he afforded no recognition at all to any forces or influences outside of himself. And the lack of recognition in our discussions for the role of any external forces, influences, or powers bespoke the absence of room in Philip's heart for the grace, blessings, and workings of the Almighty. I broached this issue carefully with Philip many times and in many ways. His most common response was "I'm one guy who really believes in the adage that God helps those who help themselves."

So despite some outward protestations to the contrary, Philip neither recognized nor paid any deference to any higher power. And his life of entitlement and self-indulgence was a clear testament to the fact that he never subordinated his will to anything or anyone bigger or greater than his own selfish desires. He actually had incredible faith, but mainly in himself. He professed to be a Christian, but he afforded no appropriate recognition to Christ or his crucial message about personal piety and righteous living. It became amply clear in our discussions that his frame of heart and mind made it impossible for him to understand, let alone appreciate, the concept that to be a true follower of the Lord, *he* (that is, his substantial ego) must diminish so that the real source of life and good in the world (that is, Christ) could increase and become manifest in him (John 3:30).

It is no accident that in the various twelve-step programs, a profession of belief in a higher power (Step 2) comes only after a person makes an admission of personal powerlessness (the all-important "First Step"). In the human heart, one cannot meaningfully embrace the hope that "God can" until one has to admit "I can't." Whatever else they might be, programs fashioned on such models are, at their very core, character development programs. And according to the tenets of Alcoholics Anonymous, "there is only one key" to the process of becoming well, "and it is called *willingness*" (Alcoholics Anonymous, *Twelve Steps and Twelve Traditions*, 34). Unfortunately, such a willingness usually only appears on the heels of total personal defeat (program participants call it "hitting bottom").

Turning oneself over to something bigger—that's what 12-step adherents know changing one's life is all about. And this turning over simply cannot be at a superficial level. For faithful program participants, it's a fully conscious and deliberate decision to surrender both mind and will to a power greater than ourselves. No more of a life based on what *we* want—only a life devoted to what that greater power wants for us. For all the criticism heaped upon such programs over the years, there is both powerful psychology and spirituality in those simple but difficult steps. And they are entirely congruent with what Jesus and his followers point to as the necessary precursors to a true change of heart.

For Philip to come to terms with what really needed to change in his life, he would have to become willing to stop charting an exclusively self-centered and self-directed course and allow himself to be guided in his actions by a greater principle. He would have to stop leading and agree to be led. For a person with an ego the size of Philip's, this is no small order under the best of circumstances, but it is virtually impossible when someone has not yet emotionally, psychologically, and spiritually hit bottom.

Of the many "Philips" with whom I have worked, only a few had suffered such complete and utter defeat or were in enough internal pain at the time of my initial contact with them that they were truly ready to undertake the task of character reconstruction. But that by no means implies a therapeutic failure in turning them away. In fact, sometimes politely declining to waste precious time and energy with someone who is not yet in the mental or emotional place to do what's necessary to change course is the single most powerful and therapeutic thing a helping professional can do. Besides, denying access to the insincere is a real power-shifter. What's more, trust, the single most important factor in solidifying a therapeutic relationship, is simply impossible to instill when a therapist or pastoral counselor appears to be "chasing after" a person who is simply not yet really ready to be guided. The Philips of this world have a sort of intuitive radar that tells them when someone else is trying harder than they are. They innately and rightfully mistrust the motives of someone too ready to embrace them when they are not really reaching out. Perhaps the therapist suffers from a hero or rescuer complex. Perhaps the person seeking counseling is more concerned about his or her reputation than whether he or she is devoted to the principles that foster genuine change. Whatever the case, it's an inevitable and irreversible trust-buster for anyone—even the most disturbed character—to sense that the person offering help possibly needs more from him or her than he or she desires at the time from a potential spiritual or psychological guide. Moreover, a therapist loses all leverage when power is tilted in favor of the impaired character (this is the exact opposite of what needs to occur in the case of counseling a troubled person of basically decent character). You can only help someone change things when he or she is truly not happy with himself or herself and ready and willing to use you as a vehicle to assist in the process of self-directed growth.

Individuals like Philip often have to be completely broken in spirit in order to be more amenable to help. And rescuing them too soon from the painful consequences of their actions can dampen what little motivation they might have. Other times, people simply have to get tired of the lying they've done to themselves, the falseness of their prior self-appraisals, and the true state of their faith. Once they sincerely admit their shortcomings and character defects, and become open to the notion that with God all things—including a much different and richer life—are possible, a door of great opportunity opens. And when they're finally ready to turn themselves over to something bigger, the work of a therapist or pastoral counselor could not be any easier, or more straightforward, pleasant, or satisfying. But that type of readiness cannot be forced, manipulated, or hastened through encouragement, cajoling, or seduction. The human heart can only open when it is ready to open. Jesus knew this well. He prefaced and concluded many parables and other teachings with phrases like "Let those with the ears to receive this teaching, hear it" or "Let those with eyes to see this, take it in." Sometimes our ears are closed and our eyes are shut. The glory of the Kingdom can be

15

blazing all about us sometimes and we simply can't perceive it because we're not spiritually, psychologically, or emotionally able to embrace it.

It was many years before Philip became truly ready for a new life in genuine faith. But when the time did come, it was clear for anyone to see. As is often the case with folks like Philip, there were some times in between when he was hurting to a substantial degree and both he and I thought he might actually be ready. But as it turned out, he hadn't yet been sufficiently defeated by his vanity to voluntarily and completely surrender it. But God would eventually permit circumstance to deal some very humbling blows to Philip. He lost his once lofty status in the community and experienced almost total financial ruin. And that's not to say that Philip didn't go kicking and screaming all the way through his custom-made ordeal. But he eventually had to acknowledge who was really in charge and held all the cards. And he had to admit how desperately he needed the Lord's firm but loving guidance. Philip would finally surrender himself to a Higher Power. And when he did, *everything* changed.

In a way, Philip's eventual "conversion" paralleled the ordeal of Saul of Tarsus: there he was, in all his righteousness, purging the ranks of a renegade sect he believed was threatening the established order and prosperity of his people. And although much of the popular lore about the events that transpired next might not be completely accurate, metaphorically, they're poetically perfect and profound: Paul simply had to get knocked off his high horse. And he had to come to terms with a very real blindness. By encountering the living Christ, he gained insight into the things with which he had really been at odds, and by entering into communion with the followers of the Light, his blindness was lifted.

It then became clear to him the direction his life would henceforth have to take. Graced with a new vision, he gladly laid down his old life and embarked upon a challenging new mission, driven not by his own self-righteous interest, but solely "by faith in the Son of God" (Galatians 2:20). And as more than two thousand years of history boldly attests to, that choice made all the difference in the world.

Philip is by no means a perfect man. But he's a much different person today than he used to be. His once pathological self-assuredness has given way to a more realistic self-assessment. And he knows how blessed he is to have had Nan stick by him, especially through his years of marginal growth. He also knows how many others he's deeply indebted to, most especially God, whom he now realizes saved him from his worst enemy: himself. There's room in Philip's heart now for much more than self-satisfaction and appreciation. He doesn't just live for himself anymore. He actually strives to do right by others. And he does his best to honor the hard lessons he's been taught and to give more than casual lip service to the faith he knows truly saved him.

When Someone Is at War with God

Some people are simply at war a lot of the time. The disposition of their hearts is such that they too often and too intensely pit themselves against others, the world at large, and most especially, authority figures. This necessarily puts them at odds with the Ultimate Authority. A small fraction of these folks are oblivious to (that is, aren't conscious of) their contentious approach to living, but the majority are very much aware. They know full well what others, society in general, and even God desire of them. And although they might reluctantly conform or accede to expectations at times, especially when it's expedient or self-serving for them to do so, they can never really find it in their hearts to subordinate themselves to anyone or anything else. They know all the rules, but they not only often see themselves as above them, they're also determined to ignore or contest them. For many years, psychologists assumed that such a hostile disposition must necessarily be the outgrowth of childhood marked by severe abuse, neglect, or heartless treatment. But evidence is mounting every day that this is not always the case. And some evidence has emerged that some of the more adamant "fighters" among us are, to a remarkable degree, naturally so inclined. But regardless of the origins of such a predisposition, the senseless warriors among us (whom I describe in my other writings as the aggressive personalities [see Simon, *Character Disturbance*, 96–128]) often cause many problems for society and inflict considerable pain on others. The vignette that follows tells a tragic tale of a man determined to have his way, regardless of the cost to others or his soul.

The Story of Larry

Larry had always been a rebel. He was the one whom the others could count on to pull amusing pranks on the teacher or dare to defy the principal. He was also a star on the basketball court and on the football field. And he was always the leader, never the follower. He dared to dress and act differently. He always did things his own way. No thinking person would challenge him to a fight. And you didn't dare cross him because you knew there would undoubtedly be some sort of hell to pay.

Larry clawed and scraped his way to a prosperous life as the owner of a small company. He made it in the business world despite having dropped out of high school (he explained many times that the teachers had it in for him, and, besides, he knew he was smarter than most of the "idiots" there and eventually "just got tired of dealing with their bull****." His business thrived, even in difficult economic times, largely because of his determination to succeed.

The fact that Larry eventually had to turn over the reins of his business and was now serving time in prison really didn't appear to bother him all that much. He knew he would survive the temporary loss of his freedom. Besides, he had become resigned to the inescapable consequences of his actions. They simply came with the territory of being caught. And he knew he could withstand what "the system" was *really* trying to do: break him, crush his confidence, make him into something he would *never* allow himself to become. So he resolved to do his time, and do it in an outwardly gracious manner besides. There was no way he was going to go through life with his head hung low. He'd rather die than surrender his pride. He would be neither humbled nor defeated by his current circumstances. And he would emerge from this ordeal just as he had from ordeals past: stronger, smarter, and even more determined to win.

Larry was incarcerated because several years earlier he was convicted of a crime he had actually perpetrated many times without detection or sanction. He had a voracious appetite for novel, kinky, raw, and forceful sex and eventually developed a habit of targeting street prostitutes. He would drug them to unconsciousness, abduct and physically assault them, and subsequently have his way with them in any imaginable way that might titillate him. He would then literally dump them out of his truck and back onto the streets where they would eventually awaken to their bruised and abused condition. He was willing to bank on the odds that someone who was of low social standing, had a shady history, and wanted no trouble with the law would probably not report him, even if they somehow had the presence of mind to piece together what had happened to them.

Shortly after coming to prison, Larry started attending a special program organized by one of the chaplains. He became a regular attendee at services, and after only a few months was baptized and accepted Christ as his personal Savior. By his own account, he was a new man, and he eventually became deeply involved in the prison ministry. He so impressed the chaplain with his fervor in recruiting other inmates that he soon became a valued assistant and trusted ally. Although some of his fellow inmates thought his lightning-fast conversion quite suspect, and surmised that his all-consuming involvement in the ministry might simply be a way out of other, less pleasant activities, others, including many among the professional and security staff, regarded him as a changed man and exemplary role model.

I first came into direct contact with Larry because he wanted something from me. He requested I make a formal recommendation to the parole board that he be considered for early release, based on his performance in a treatment program as well as his religious conversion. And it was clear from the tone of his request that he fully expected I would comply. After all, he noted, he had perfect attendance in his treatment classes and groups, had fulfilled all of the program's technical requirements, turned in all of his assignments, and by regulation, had been awarded a certificate of successful completion. He also noted the ardent support of the chaplain, who had already written a letter on his behalf, as well as the support of others who had come to regard him as a model prisoner. His expecting me to rubber-stamp his request meant it was inevitable that a war would ensue when I did not immediately accede to his wishes.

There was ample evidence that Larry's performance in the treatment program was as empty of substance as his newly proclaimed faith. Yes, he said a lot of the right words. He even did most of the right things. But the attitudes, patterns of thinking, and most especially, his style of relating to others (which, by definition, marked his personality) strongly suggested that he had experienced no fundamental change of heart. A telltale indication of his lack of genuine remorse for his crimes surfaced during one encounter with me when he was agitatedly challenging my admitted hesitation to send a positive letter to the parole board. How could I not be swayed by the fact that he had been "robbed of precious years of his life" and also "had to live with" the consequences of his "mistakes" every day, he queried? He also lamented how unfair it was that others, who had done far worse things, including murder, might actually serve less time than he might have to serve. In short, he was feeling sorry for himself. He was also casting himself as the real victim and playing for sympathy. And as if he hadn't been abused enough by his loss of liberty, now, despite completing a treatment program and even being born again as a Christian, he was probably going to be victimized even more by an uncaring professional balking at helping him gain the early release he believed he so rightly deserved! How, he queried, could I be so insensitive to his plight?

The fact that Larry had the audacity to accuse me of having no empathy for his circumstance and thus victimizing him in some way drew my attention to the very issue that bothered me most about him. Not once during his extensive treatment did he ever demonstrate the slightest bit of sincere empathy or genuine sorrow for the trauma he had inflicted on the true victims of his actions. In fact, there was ample evidence that he continually denigrated their characters, even after completing the paper requirements for the empathy-training component of his treatment. During his group sessions, he repeatedly referred to his victims as "whores, sluts, and addicts," and downplayed the level of harm he caused them. He cast them as no-accounts whose lives were already shipwrecks. And although he would frequently assert that he'd taken responsibility for his actions, he neither admitted to nor expressed regret for the most vile and well-documented aspects of his crimes. He even had the nerve to blame one of his victims for instigating the most egregious and merciless of his attacks. His lack of genuine remorse for his actions or empathy for his victims was clearly evident in all of his encounters with me. The only concern he ever expressed was for himself. To me it seemed clear: he wasn't truly repentant, wasn't sufficiently rehabilitated (as evidenced by the fact that neither his manner of thinking nor his manner of behaving was any different after treatment compared to before), and therefore could not possibly be a new man in the faith he so strongly protested he'd found.

During his treatment, Larry outwardly acceded to the literal demands placed upon him (this is known as the tactic of "giving assent" [Simon, *Character Disturbance*, 187]), but all of his actions indicated that he never took to heart the most fundamental principles the program advocated. As is the case in many such programs, he had been urged to: (1) cease "objectifying," degrading, and dehumanizing others; (2) challenge and change his attitudes and ways of thinking about how a person should go about getting the things he or she wants in this world; (3) be sensitive to and respect the rights and concerns of others; (4) take ownership of his decisions and actions; (5) discipline his appetites and temper his urges; and (6) cultivate a sufficient degree of empathy toward others that he might be deterred from doing in the future the kinds of heartless things he'd done in the past. Despite all of his rhetoric, Larry never bought into the central tenets of the philosophy to which he was exposed. And his behavior with me during the several meetings we had clearly demonstrated that he had failed to take any of the aforementioned principles to heart.

Just as Larry hadn't taken to heart the values promoted in his treatment program, he also hadn't really embraced the core creeds of the Christian faith. In so many ways and on so many levels—but most especially because of his incapacity to heed Christ's command to love—Larry was *not* a believer. One might rightfully ponder how such a situation can occur. He was baptized by an ordained minister, reborn into a new life in the Lord. He had confessed with his lips and in the presence of many his acceptance of Christ as his personal savior. How could he not be saved? But even more important, how could someone purportedly saved remain as wily, defiant, and possibly dangerous as ever?

Now I know that many would assert that acknowledging Christ's saving act is all that is necessary for salvation and that Larry's continued malice of heart—a by-product of his inherently flawed human nature—is irrelevant to the issue of being saved. I have heard this argument many times before. And this same issue was the subject of debate between the newcomer to the faith, Paul, and the Apostle James, almost two thousand years ago. But as James so rightly pointed out, the controversy is really a false one because it's simply impossible to separate genuine faith from the righteousness it inexorably must engender (the whole of James 2). Our real faith, James asserts, is revealed not by the verbal claims

23

we make but rather by the actions we take. And although our works do not have the power to make us clean of heart and justified before God, the leap of faith that ultimately saves us can only be taken by the willing heart.

Larry's case demonstrates clearly the relative meaninglessness of verbal professions of belief (treatment program veterans affectionately refer to this as the difference between "talking the talk" and "walking the walk"). And just as James asserted all those years ago and years of modern behavioral science have confirmed through research, a person's fundamental and most genuine beliefs are revealed most accurately not by their words but by their actions. Larry never experienced the change of heart and mind or *metanoia* that defines real conversion. That can only happen when a person deliberately puts ego in its place (Zweig and Abrams, *Meeting the Shadow*, 109) and voluntarily surrenders to something bigger. Unfortunately, Larry still walks the same walk he always has.

Larry's true character came more clearly to the fore when I didn't join the chorus of those endorsing his status as changed man. Fighter that he is, he eventually brought out some big guns in his bid to overcome all resistance to an early release. He solicited more letters from his chaplain and the chaplain's colleagues, sought the intercession of a politically well-connected friend of his family, procured a petition from a member of the hierarchy of a certain religious denomination, found the ear of a state senator, lodged a formal complaint with my superiors, and even threatened legal action against me and the institution. He was determined to have what he believed he deserved, despite no meaningful evidence that he had earned the privilege. All of his actions were consistent with the type of personality he had always had. He was still at war with the world and its rules, and at war with me simply because he saw me as an obstacle between him and something he wanted. But it takes at least two to conduct a real war, and it took all my resolve to refrain from participating in the conflict. I promised myself not to argue with him and I didn't attempt to persuade him to change course. I simply wouldn't acquiesce to his demands. And while Larry would cast this as a hostile act on my part (whether he truly viewed it in that manner is subject to debate), I simply couldn't accede to his wishes because I had already subordinated myself to a principle higher than his selfish desire.

The real Larry would eventually become known even to those whom he had for a time deceived. And as fate would have it, he ended up not only serving his entire sentence but also incurring additional time on new charges. It came to light that he'd been conducting a scam that involved stealing personal identity information he'd come across while lending his accounting expertise to help various corrections employees do their tax returns (this was against the rules regarding fraternization, of course, but reflects the degree to which folks had come to trust his rhetoric about his newfound faith—even to the degree that they were willing to set aside their better judgment). When his con game was exposed, these individuals felt quite betrayed. In their hearts, they wanted to believe that Larry had changed because he'd said and done so many of the right things many God-fearing folks believe mark a person who's been saved. But they didn't look for the right things. Nothing had ever really changed at the core with Larry. He never gave himself away and picked up Christ. And the most important signs indicating that were *everywhere*. They simply weren't given the proper notice or afforded the right degree of importance because of the misguided notions so many of us harbor about what it really means for a person to be born again in spirit. This is a most important concept to understand and accept. When people really change, there are unmistakable signs of it. And I believe I have encountered many people, even serious wrongdoers, whose newfound faith has changed their hearts and completely turned their lives around. But the difference in such folks is unmistakable. They don't feel the same way, think the same way, and most especially, don't act the same way they once did. It's not that they talk a good line, it's that they evidence a whole new way of being.

To this day, Larry remains very much a man at war. He's still at war with "the system" that sought to punish him for pain he caused others (he spends many hours in the prison law library researching possible technical errors and other avenues for release). He's at war with society because he knows it's trying to change him from the person he is determined to remain. And he's ultimately at war with God because even though the chaplain's once-frequent counsel made it clear to him what the Lord desires, Larry cannot conceive of a life worth living that's not lived on *his* terms and with *him* clearly in the driver's seat. That's what made Larry's testimony about being saved so empty and meaningless in the first place. James challenged the earliest Christians to keep in mind that the tongue is just as capable of cursing our brothers as it is of praising the Almighty, and it is also prone to boasting (James 3). You simply cannot trust the tongue, he argued, and the only thing really capable of guiding us to truth and righteousness is a spirit surrendered to and in communion with God. Real faith transforms us in spirit. And the condition of our spirit is always reflected in the love we display as opposed to what we say we believe. How easy it is to *say* we believe! But oh how hard it is to act in a manner that demonstrates we've really yielded our hearts and minds to our professed convictions.

For the truly believing person, terms like being "saved" and "born again" should really mean something. Being born again is a really big deal. A person can be immersed in three rivers of water and be no more made anew than a marble statue. When John the Baptist was conducting his ministry by the Jordan River, he urged others to proclaim by the sign of washing themselves in the flowing waters that they meant to cleanse themselves of and repent of their sins, and to turn their minds and hearts to the Lord (Mark 1:4-6 and John). He also proclaimed, according to the Aramaic account, that whereas he had immersed people in water, Christ would immerse people in the Spirit of Holiness, never again to be the same. Being born again in spirit is a much more momentous event than the difficult task of turning over one's "mind and will" to a higher power, as 12-step program adherents strive to do. It is life on a whole new plane, lived by a guiding principle completely unnatural to the human psyche (Rohr, *The Naked Now*, 89–91).

The thing that can really get to you when you hear stories like Larry's is that because Christ is always present, knocking on the door to our hearts in so many different ways, it's so profoundly tragic when someone professes to accept and welcome him, yet slams the door squarely in his face. Christ was seeking entry into Larry's heart during every pastoral counseling session he attended, every therapy group he participated in, and in every encounter he had with those who held such high hope that he was truly about the business of changing his stripes. But despite his outward protests to the contrary, Larry had really only stiffened his resolve and his general approach to life. No matter how many times he touted his baptismal ritual, Larry never even wanted, let alone adopted, a new life. He wanted his old one, but this time on steroids! He wanted to live his life on his own terms and no one else's, not even the Lord's. So he placed his faith where he always had: in himself and his uncanny ability to con (that is, manipulate the impression of) others. He also believed he could do his jail time in record time and with minimal discomfort. And he almost succeeded in this effort. Fortunately, for all of us, the Lord always has the final say.

In view of the many misconceptions that abound when it comes to understanding folks like Larry, I think it's important to say something about his background. He was raised in a most faithful Christian household. Both of his parents are righteous and God-fearing people. He was neither traumatized nor indulged during his upbringing. His unique attributes and defects of character belong solely to him. Yet his parents, most especially his mother, can't help questioning and faulting themselves even to this day. I've seen this kind of psychological dynamic too many times, and it is always unnerving. Sometimes, when others in a family harbor so much conscience, a child can lack the incentive to develop much of a conscience of his or her own. And if the child happens to be a natural-born "fighter," like Larry, that child tends from his or her earliest days to fight the socialization process that parents, teachers, and others impose upon him or her in any way possible, making it even more difficult to develop an adequate conscience.

If ever a person needed to be born again, it would be someone like Larry. But the mere words and rituals of baptism are not enough to accomplish this. The best hope for persons like Larry is abundant love and unwavering, courageous honesty. But often, such folks are not yet in a mental, emotional, or spiritual place to recognize, receive, or respond to either. Unable to embrace the promise of love (and therefore unable to accept Christ, the very personification of perfect love), they place their faith in *power* as the surest means of advancing their interests (Ruiz, *The Mastery of Love*, 89), and often resort to impression-management and other types of manipulation to secure that power in their encounters with others. Still, because they are so deeply familiar with and skilled in dishonesty, they can readily recognize—although they don't always appreciate—honesty in others. Only honest engagement coupled with resolute, steadfast, and plentiful love can help them come to believe in something different. And misplaced compassion, wishful thinking, and abandonment of accountability on the part of others are no substitute for the kind of love they really need. Still, it's no joy when the most loving thing you can do at a particular point in time is to say no to them. Doing the right thing almost always comes with a steep cost and incurs adverse consequences. For a while, Larry made my life quite difficult. It's simply not easy to love a guy like Larry.

When a Person Abuses in the Name of God

The Lord commands that we hold his Name in complete and solemn reverence. That means we should never use it casually or for any untoward or self-serving purpose. Unfortunately, I've met many individuals who engage in all sorts of self-serving, unseemly behavior in the Lord's name, and who cloak all manner of ruthlessness under the guise of heeding the Lord's bidding. Invoking the name of God to manipulatively advance one's own nefarious agendas is an egregious sin that is common to a particular disturbed character type. The following story is an example.

The Story of Ted and Teri

Ted was one of the most active persons in his congregation and was regarded by many as a staunch defender of the faith. He was admired as both a leader and an organizer, and he had spurred several of his friends and acquaintances into more active involvement in the church's activities over the years. He seemed a tireless worker for the Lord. He attended services every week, was active in Bible study, and could cite Bible chapter and verse with the best of them. Ted appeared every bit a decent, Christian man.

His reputation in the church and community was just one of the things that made Teri so self-doubting the first time she tried to confront Ted about his domineering and controlling ways. Over the years, she had increasingly come to see Ted not so much as God-fearing and God-serving, but rather ruthlessly self-serving and unyielding. And although they always toed the line, even Ted's and Teri's kids were becoming increasingly unnerved by him and had begun to distance themselves from him. Ted's flares of temper when someone didn't do as he thought he or she should were becoming more frequent and intense. Teri was quite worried about what things would come to if this continued, so she worked up the courage to address the issues with him.

Teri tried to approach Ted with her concerns in as nonthreatening a manner as possible. She suggested the possibility of counseling, which he seemed open to at first. He even admitted that on occasion he might have gone too far in expressing his displeasure or in meting out punishments to the children. And for a while, it would appear he was making an effort to do better. Then he would begin balking at the notion of seeking help, and when an episode occurred, would only lament that if he could only get those in his family to "do right," and to "honor the Lord's will," he'd never have reason to get upset.

For most of their marriage, Ted appeared deeply devoted, though undoubtedly strict. But his sternness never took the form of violence. He just seemed to be fiercely dedicated to doing right and upholding noble standards for his family, wanting the best out of and for his wife and children. So even when family members bristled under the weight of his condemning demeanor and harsh dictates, they believed he was only trying to be a good man and doing his best to instill the highest respect for God's will. It was only in recent years that his behavior was appearing more abusive than convicted. And the more Teri brought his behavior to his attention, the more verbally and emotionally abusive Ted became, going on ever more frequent tirades, and always berating her and the children for causing his distress in the first place and triggering his anger.

Eventually, Ted's outbursts got so frequent and so intense that both Teri and the kids were becoming afraid. And when he was confronted about it, all he could do was point a finger at them, claiming it was they who had actually gotten worse in their disregard for the Lord's will. Even his initial apparent willingness to get some help had faded. Teri finally decided she'd had enough and threw down the gauntlet. And it would be the first time in her marriage that she dared to set forth her own demands. Nonetheless, she made her wishes clear to Ted: either he would receive counseling and get to the root of what she saw as his anger issues or she would leave him. In the meantime, she would make arrangements so that she and the children could live temporarily with her sister, until it was clear that Ted was making some progress in therapy and the family had some reason to hope that things were going to be different.

Once Teri took her stand, she would soon come to learn not only who Ted really was, but what can happen when someone like Ted is held to account for their issues. He became more openly intimidating than ever once Teri actually began making plans to live with her sister for a while. He would frequently question her in a style resembling a police interrogation and grill her over whether she wasn't planning to simply end their marriage anyway. And he warned her that if she actually did separate from him, he'd be sure to leave her in dire financial straits and see to it she would never get custody of the children. When Teri called him on these intimidation tactics, he immediately fired back, blaming her outright for everything, and insisting that the wound she had inflicted on him by even suggesting the renunciation of her marriage vows was the root cause of all his pain and righteous anger. When she wouldn't accept that notion (which she knew to be not only factually inaccurate but probably also bogus), he invited her to strike him. After all, he taunted, she had already thrust an emotional knife deep into his heart. A physical strike would pale in comparison to the damage she'd already done. At least that's what he wanted her to believe. And when Teri, in understandable fear of the escalating rhetoric and passion Ted was displaying, walked away, he shoved her. In that moment, almost everything became clear to Teri. Ted was capable of almost anything when his will was thwarted. This shook her to her foundations, and later that day she and the children left for her sister's.

There are people in this world whose main concern is being on top and in control. As long as they have their way, they're content. But try to stand on equal ground with them, or resist acceding to their demands, and there's bound to be trouble. I'm not talking here about people who conscientiously, and with respect for boundaries and limits, know how to take care of and assert themselves. Rather, I'm talking about those among us who pursue what they want without sufficient regard for the impact on others. Some of these folks are openly and unashamedly aggressive in their manner: they brazenly weave through traffic, always alert for the patrol car that might impede them; look forward to wrestling with demons at work; enjoy decimating their competitors in business as well as at play; and are forever determined to have the upper hand in any interpersonal encounter. But others, though just as aggressive, do their best to conceal their true nature and principal agendas. They might portray themselves as caring, dutiful, and upright or even charming and likable while using a variety of tactics to subtly run roughshod over others by playing on their conscientiousness, accepting natures, fears, or insecurities. They are the archetypal wolves in sheep's clothing (Simon, *In Sheep's Clothing*, 46) and who they really are usually comes to light only when their tactics of manipulating and controlling others begin to fail.

Ted's favorite manipulation tactics had always been invoking the name of the Lord, quoting Scripture, and using his purported commitment to his faith as weapons of coercion and control. Display any resistance to his expressed wishes, and you could count on him to eventually bring out his spiritual trump cards. Neither Teri nor the children regarded these things as tactics for most of the years they'd been together. They bought into the notion that he was a stern but nonetheless righteous and dedicated man with unusually high standards who ultimately just wanted the best for everyone. And they believed he was only trying to exercise the spiritual leadership he believed he was obliged to show as the titular head of a Christian household. But Ted never really understood the nature of real leadership. He didn't put his energy into a loving example that almost anyone might feel inspired to emulate. Rather, he tried to impose his will in the most devious and subtle ways possible. His family eventually came to see this purported man of God as a primal power-luster in disguise. And once Teri finally had Ted's number and called him on it, he allowed his once carefully crafted veil of civility to drop and abandoned his usual, more subtle tactics for more overt intimidation and threats.

Very few Christians really understand the third (by some accounts, the second) utterance of God to Moses. After God introduced himself, he commanded the children of Israel to afford their utmost reverence to his very identity (Christ himself affirms this in the opening lines of the Lord's Prayer [Matthew 6:9; Luke 11:2]). He decreed that his Name not only be held sacred but also never be uttered with any prideful or base intention. Not taking the Name of the Lord thy God in vain is much more than not cursing or uttering forms of it in exclamations of hate, disgust, or frustration. It's never using God's great and supremely good name for any mundane, pointless, or most especially, self-serving purpose. Although no one in the family had ever heard him curse, Ted had been taking and using the name of God in vain for years. He brought God into everything, though not in a benign or loving way.

For many years Ted appeared to be only honoring a steadfast commitment to doing God's will. But it would be fair to say that Ted actually "used" God as a vehicle for wielding tyranny in his home. Ted was in fact a person who subordinated himself to no one, not even God, and attempted to rule over his subjects with an iron fist. Although he cast himself as submitting to the Lord's will, there was not a submissive bone in Ted's body. And the fact that he would temporarily yield when his tyrannical ways threatened the dissolution of everything he valued testifies not only to how aware he was and how intentional his actions were but also to how much control he could exercise over them if he so chose. Moreover, the fact that he quickly returned to his domineering ways whenever the specter of loss dissipated for a time demonstrates how insincere he was about really addressing the problem.

Aggressive personalities come in various shapes and sizes (Simon, *Character Disturbance*, 96), but they all have the same crucial character flaw: they so abhor the notion of *submission*—to anyone or anything—that they will go to extraordinary lengths to resist it. While it's relatively easy to recognize those who are open and brazen in their desire to dominate, it's much harder to get an accurate read on those adept at the art of cloaking their hunger to control under the guise of almost anything else. And as we have seen exemplified time and time again in the cases of disgraced and money-hungry televangelists, there is almost no more effective, albeit reprehensible, way for someone to veil their aggressive nature or intentions and manipulate those with kind and innocent hearts than to don the cloak of religiosity. Covert-aggression in the name of the Lord is a serious and age-old problem. The history of humankind is replete with instances of untold misery inflicted on innocent men, women, and children by power-seekers invoking the name of, and claiming only service to, the Almighty.

It's a common, but from my experience, erroneous, notion that folks like Ted struggle with anger issues that they need to get under better control. Deal with the underlying anger, learn to manage it, and things will be better, so the popular wisdom goes. This was Teri's presumption as well. But people like Ted don't really need, nor do they profit much from, anger management. That's because anger is not the *cause* of their problems. Rather, it's both the *result* and a cardinal sign (that is, an objectively observable phenomenon that fairly definitively indicates the presence of a specific type of pathology) of the real problem. The real problem is Ted's excessive and unrelenting aggressive predisposition. What's more, the behavior of aggressive personalities is rarely driven by anger. Rather, for the most part, they are motivated by raw and unbridled desire. They simply want what they want. It's when they feel denied, encounter resistance, or don't immediately succeed in satisfying their wishes then they become irritated and angry. And the fact that they so frequently display their upset is a testament not only to how poorly they handle the reality that not every human desire is meant to be fully or immediately satisfied but also how often they are locked into aggressive modes of behavior. These types of personalities are always going after something. And they don't easily take no for an answer.

When Teri came to the point that she truly believed they must separate, at least for a time, it was no accident that Ted played the ultimate "God" card. He knew Teri very well. She was a dutiful, devoted, and God-fearing wife and mother. She had the most genuine commitment to the well-being of her family. So it was logical for him to try to persuade her to stay by constantly promoting the notion that because God had brought them together in the first place, a betrayal of her marriage vow of "for better or for worse" would be the ultimate act of rejection of her religious principles, and that she certainly would be held accountable by God for the "deadly sin" she was contemplating. For a while, this and similar tactics on Ted's part worked. But in the end, they failed. And when all his covert tactics had become ineffective, he dropped the pretense of civility completely, becoming only overt in his threats (for example, threats to sue for sole custody of the children and deny Teri access, threats to crucify her in court as an unfit mother, threats to trash her reputation among family and friends, and threats to leave her destitute).

Perhaps nothing revealed the true nature of Ted's character and the emptiness of his professed faith more than the manner in which he behaved when the reality of how likely he was to lose Teri finally sunk in. For the first few days after she and the kids moved out, he was as hostile and defiant as ever. But sensing the real possibility of losing his family, and despite the abuse he had already heaped upon Teri that would necessarily dampen anyone's level of compassion for him, he began begging, pleading, and playing the plaintive, suffering card. Then, for a few weeks, he was like a lamb. He even found a therapist and started going to sessions. After each session, he would declare to Teri the wonderful insights he had gained and how eager he was to make amends. Still, it wasn't long before he began putting subtle pressure on her to avoid any serious consideration about dissolving the marriage until she saw the new man he was sure to become. And as was typical for him, his patience wore thin when Teri didn't immediately signal an eagerness to move back. Once again, he became more open and forceful in his demands. Why not move back home and work things out? Why alienate the kids? Wasn't it enough that he was finally getting help? They could start going to marriage enhancement meetings at the church. He was doing something she wanted. Now, shouldn't she be giving some ground?

Ted's insincerity about changing his ways became even more

evident when, after only six counseling sessions (and Teri had still not acceded to any of his wishes), he stated there was no use in trying anymore and declared he would sue for divorce himself. He bemoaned that Teri was never the kind of wife or mother his faith taught him to value, and vowed once again that he would not only take custody of the children but also would be sure to leave Teri without a penny. This was the real Ted: a determined and unscrupulous fighter, cloaked for much of his life in the robe of a deeply religious man, willing to abandon that cloak in a heartbeat when it no longer served his wishes.

It's in the very nature of aggressive personalities, including the covertly aggressive variety like Ted, to defer to no one, not even God. But they are prone to use God, like they use everything else: as a vehicle to get what they want. This is a hard thing to see, because their charade of masking their power hunger under the guise of conviction can be both convincing and effective. They can appear to be persons of extraordinary faith. But when God is not really at the center of one's spiritual life, all the religious symbolic trappings in the world cannot hide the fact that genuine faith is lacking or absent.

Aggressive personalities are naturally inclined toward leadership positions. They want to be in the driver's seat, set the course, and call the shots. And they expect others to follow. But Christ taught us that spiritual leadership can only come from a dedication to selfless service and a commitment to serve the cause of the Lord of Life. Christ demonstrated this in vivid fashion when he knelt before his disciples to wash their feet (John 13:5-8). Peter, thinking like a typical human leader, thought the move beneath Jesus and balked at the notion of having him wash his feet, as both a way of showing respect and sparing Jesus what he regarded as humiliation. But Jesus rebuked Peter in a most stunning way, and humbled him as well by suggesting that anyone not respecting the nobility of his role as servant really didn't understand him and didn't have the kind of relationship with him they might have thought they had. He also suggested that the apostles didn't yet understand the nature of real leadership, and provided them with a poignant example.

Self-righteous, sanctimonious people simply can't be truly righteous people. Of all the things Christ sent resounding messages about, there is nothing he called attention to more frequently than the fallacy of equating righteousness with extremism, insensitivity, indifference, and power-seeking under the guise of devotion and adherence to the law. This was the substance of his most frequent and scathing criticism of the scribes and Pharisees. The rules, he argued, are fundamentally there for humans' benefit, not vice versa (Mark 2:27). Of course he was not advocating that humans simply disregard the rules by which we need to live. But he was making a statement about the nature of the rules and the righteousness they are meant to foster. And as he went about doing the essential work of his father, everything he did was righteous, even if he happened to violate or sidestep a minor detail of the law. This always upset the Pharisees, who judged only certain particulars of his conduct. Christ's judgment, however, was of the Pharisees' hearts. Purity is determined not by what substance might be taken in but rather by the substance of what emanates from the human heart. Christ's purity was as blazing white as the sun itself when he healed on the Sabbath, but the light could not be appreciated by those who saw only darkness in his disregard for the traditional ban on work. There are plenty of Pharisees still among us. They are the pretentious lot who proclaim the Lord's will from the rooftops, expect everyone to step in line, blame others' misfortune on their unworthiness, and feel vindicated in their stance when good things happen to come their way.

Christ is a living example of the righteous life. He was familiar with and intimately understood the entire and essential substance of Jewish law and the wisdom of the prophets when he commanded us to love the Lord our God with our whole hearts, our whole minds, and our whole strength as well as to love our neighbors as ourselves. And he promised that loving with the intensity and quality he advocated is what real living is all about. The message is actually quite straightforward and simple. Unfortunately, as most of us know, it's particularly difficult to follow. And for some personalities, especially those who are inclined toward power and control, it's an almost impossible task. Such folks simply can't place their faith in something greater, and they can't "let go and let God." They resist turning over the governance of their hearts, minds, and energy to the only one who should reign supreme. The truly righteous life is not one proudly boasted of as rigidly lived in accordance with religious precepts, but one in which the spirit of the law is humbly manifested in all of one's actions.

Ted was a believer in neither the Christ (the very embodiment of love) nor his message of unwavering love. And it was not Christ's will that he wanted to see done. Rather, it was his own will he wanted enforced, and he was willing to play on the God-fearing nature of those around him as insurance that he would be obeyed. Despite all his protests to the contrary, his was *not* a God-centered life but a self-centered one, and in the end, his will to dominate cost him everything of value that he had ever had. He lost a fine woman, Teri, and although he was awarded joint custody of his children, their estrangement from him would only increase over the years. They eventually came to know another father figure whose arms were much more open to them just as they are than their father's arms ever were. Make no mistake Ted's children have always been wonderful persons—smart, dutiful, and honorable. And they have always been faithful to the essential Christian principles of living. They have not only honored their father with their lives, just as the commandment requires, but they also have never stopped truly loving him. However, they simply can't endure too much exposure to his destructive energy. So they have to enforce some reasonable limits and boundaries in their contacts with him—a sad case, indeed.

I've known a lot of people like Ted. In fact, I wrote a book about them. They're among the most problematic personalities you'll ever meet and can bring an extraordinary amount of turmoil, confusion, and pain into your life. But not all of them were as resistant to change as Ted. Sometimes, God was merciful enough to allow the costs of their behavior to rise so high that they were finally forced to question their way of doing things. Other times, enough people became clued in to their real natures that they were forced to abandon their sham facade. Circumstances can indeed sometimes soften the hardest of hearts. But to really change for the better, folks like Ted have to come to a place where they can be truthful about their underlying motivations and behavior. Jesus had it absolutely right: the truth has the power to set us free (John 8:32), if only we have the courage to face it and the integrity to admit it. So there is an antidote to the disease of sanctimonious self-righteousness: the courage to call someone out on their real agenda.

CHAPTER 2

WHEN WELL-INTENTIONED, BASICALLY GOOD PEOPLE DO HARM

One of life's most sobering realities is that often it simply isn't enough to mean well when we're trying to address and solve our problems. In our ignorance, what we sometimes think is the most rational or caring course can ultimately turn out to be the most damaging action we could have taken. Over the many years that I've counseled individuals, couples, and families, I've unfortunately witnessed many cases in which decent people, with the very best of intentions, ended up doing more harm than good when trying to make a situation better.

When Someone Does Too Much

Sometimes a person can do so much for another person that the other person has little incentive to do very much for herself or himself. I've seen this happen all too many times. Often, a parent who is overly conscientious becomes so mindful of his or her child's needs and attends to the child so dutifully that he or she never acquires sufficient motivation to develop his or her own sense of industriousness. Of course, it's not that the parent wants to harm the child. On the contrary, the parent's usual motivation is genuine concern for the child's welfare. And when a child is innately prone to be inordinately negligent and reckless, a parent can easily develop a greater than normal level of concern. But when an excessively worried parent ends up doing far too much to stave off disaster, it can, at least in part, diminish the chances the child will ever do what's necessary to properly tend to his or her own well-being.

The Story of Martha and David

When you pressed her on the matter, Martha might be willing to admit that she probably cared about her son David a bit too much. And under the right circumstances, she might even admit why she felt compelled to do so much for him. Martha had always felt that David was cut a bad deal in life. His father died when David was very young, and because Martha was hesitant to remarry and there were no other father figures available to him within the extended family, David never had a significant adult male presence in his life. Martha not only felt bad about this but also felt partly to blame. At times, she'd considered remarrying just to provide David with an adult male role model. But there were many reasons she was unsure about entering into a new relationship. Still, she felt as if she had cheated David in some way.

Martha didn't feel bad for David just because he didn't have a father. He had also suffered more than his fair share of other misfortunes. While he was still in high school, David sustained a severe leg injury as the result of an accident in a car his friend was driving. This left him unable to play the sports he once so dearly cherished and also ended any hopes he might have had to play college football. Martha knew David mourned this loss and she felt bad for him. But what pained her even more was the fact that just weeks before his wedding date, David's fiancée called off their engagement. This not only put an end to the longest and most decent relationship David ever had with a woman but also broke his heart. For so many reasons, Martha felt David had experienced more than his fair share of disappointment in life. That's what made it so hard for her not to care as much about him as she did.

Martha would not deny that David had some long-standing behavioral problems. He had shown much irresponsibility in several areas of his life. He dropped out of school, had a history of being unreliable and not showing up at work, and for years had been abusing alcohol and other drugs. Martha had been aware of how serious David's alcohol and drug use was for some time. She also felt that these behaviors were at the root of many of his other problems. And it's not like she hadn't tried to get him help. In fact, she'd gone through all of her deceased husband's life insurance money and most of her own savings just to pay all the costs the medical plan wouldn't cover for David's multiple stints in rehab.

Martha would reluctantly admit that she simply didn't have the heart to let David hit bottom as several of his treatment counselors said he'd probably have to do before turning his life around. After all he'd already been through, how could she let him sink to that level of despair? He had already suffered more than enough pain and misfortune in his life. She just couldn't stand for him to be in any more misery. So when he wrecked his car, she had it repaired. When he defaulted on his rent, she paid it. And when he got into scrapes with the law, she got the best legal assistance she could find to get him out of hot water. Martha always did whatever it took to provide David the support she thought he needed.

I first became acquainted with David and his mother during one of his many admissions to an inpatient substance abuse treatment program. I was on staff at the hospital that housed the program and one of the counselors asked if I would render an opinion about the overall assessment of matters and provide some adjunctive therapy services. Because David had recently become a legal adult, I had to secure his permission for the consultation, which he granted. And, as always, Martha readily indicated her willingness to be an active part of whatever treatment I might deem necessary. After all, family participation is what the program coordinators always said was such an important part of therapy. But it didn't take me long to realize who was investing the most time or energy in the enterprise. Whereas David was often late for groups, forgot or didn't complete his assignments, and had to be roused from bed to attend activities, Martha was prompt, attentive, and fully engaged in all the events designed for family participation.

Although Martha faithfully attended every family therapy session, participated in all the discussion and support groups, and knew the tenets of the program backward and forward, many of the other group participants felt she didn't seem to "get it" with respect to her own dependency issues. She was confronted about this many times in various group sessions. To some, it seemed she just didn't understand the adverse impact of her over-investment in David's welfare. But it would soon become clear to me how much Martha actually did understand, at least on an intellectual level. In spite of her intellectual awareness, on an emotional level, Martha simply wasn't prepared to let go.

I remember well the impressions I formed during the first occasion I met with David alone. He appeared to express not only some amusement but also some disdain for his mother's well-known and intense involvement in his treatment. On one hand, he gave the impression he was entertained by the notion that she would make herself jump through all sorts of hoops on his behalf. It was one of the few things that made him feel somewhat special and important. On the other hand, it really seemed to unnerve him on some level that his mother appeared so willing to put herself out to such a degree. It appeared as if she were demeaning herself. He knew very well he wasn't worthy of such an inordinate level of fidelity and devotion. And while he believed his mother to be a decent person who deeply cared for him, he could not really respect her for selling herself so woefully short.

I once challenged David about why he might not necessarily feel some sense of obligation to prove that he was worth all the fuss his mother had always made over him. I challenged him on other matters too, but David's initial response to my challenges was minimal and devoid of any passion. So, fairly quickly, one of the issues that would have to be a primary focus of our work became abundantly clear: David had become quite accustomed to doing very little, and I would have to be very tactful in finding ways to encourage him to do more, while being careful not to do too much myself.

David once plainly admitted that a big reason he never had to do much for himself was because his mother was always so willing to do so much for him. He also admitted that because he felt so smacked around by life on so many occasions, he didn't know if he could ever muster the motivation to really invest himself in anything. Putting his heart into something and then taking the chance he might fail would only invite heartbreak. But even more interestingly, David acknowledged that after years of doing so little, and with his mother always picking up after him, he had actually come to feel fairly inept. He simply hadn't learned the art of reckoning with defeat, picking himself up after failure, and starting over. In fact, David had few survival and self-advancement skills. He had even poorer social interaction skills. He was a young adult with the skills of a small child. And his biggest claim to fame was knowing how to brandish such superficial charm and play the victim role with such finesse that tender-hearted folks might jump over hurdles to play nursemaid to him. David's ex-fiancée played this role for a while until she'd had enough of it, and the string of girlfriends he'd had since the engagement ended were manipulated into this role as he led them to try extra hard to cut through the indifference he showed them. Even though at some level he hated both them and himself for it, it nonetheless made him feel like somebody to have others, especially women, dote on him. He knew that if he were to feel worthwhile in any legitimate way, he'd have to put forth much more effort than he had for many years. And given his track record of loss and failure, he simply wasn't willing to take the chance that he might try and fail, or that life might deal him yet another major blow.

Learning what a faithless person David had become was more than a bit sobering. To David, it seemed like about the only things he felt he could really count on were the proverbial black cloud he thought had been hovering over him for most of the last seven years, his mother's unwavering devotion, and the alcohol and drugs that he had come to believe were his most reliable friends and sources of comfort. His substances always seemed to be there for him, easing his pain, and doing exactly what he wanted them to do and as immediately as he wanted them to do it. Encouraging him to abandon these untrustworthy and destructive friends, stop leaning on and taking advantage of his mother, and place his trust in the true Source of power to provide him the strength to stand on his own was a most daunting task. But I knew I'd only be revealing my own deficiencies of faith if I succumbed to feeling so sorry for him that I failed to challenge him to do exactly that. I certainly didn't want to become just one more of David's many enablers.

My work with David was lengthy and exacting but not arduous or taxing. The most difficult part was being patient, maintaining the proper pace, and investing only the minimum amount of energy necessary to prompt change. The burden would have to remain largely on David and he would have to experience small, steady successes in addition to some failures. And it would be some time before he found the value in his effort. For far too long in his life, David had felt like he had servants (his mother, at one time, his fiancée, and, in a certain odd sense, even his drugs) working for him. And while that gave him a sense of worth, underneath it all, he felt like a failure and knew he was no more than a slave to his addictions. So providing just the right encouragement for him to take the frequent proverbial leaps he needed to take, risk failure, and in the process find his faith and courage was a challenge indeed. But as challenging as it was, my work with David did not turn out to be as difficult as I initially anticipated. Once he got past the notion that the advice I gave him to acknowledge even the smallest efforts on his part was neither trite nor useless, he readily regained a sense of personal power and worth. And he would eventually reclaim his faith as well, especially after coming to believe that the ordeal that was helping him reclaim that sense of worth must actually have been a blessing from a God who had never given up hope on him.

Working with Martha, and encouraging her to quit doing so much and trying so hard to prop up her son in the hope he might possibly one day magically stumble upon his own strength was much more challenging. Martha initially viewed me as the most heartless mental health professional she'd ever met. Plus, she felt insulted that I appeared critical and possibly even condemning of her care and concern for her son. It was a sizable undertaking to help her differentiate between the sincerity and possibly even nobility of her intentions and the inherent destructiveness of her actions. Only when the issues of faith that were clearly at the root of her family's problems were openly discussed and confronted did Martha begin to see both the love and the wisdom behind the counsel I was attempting to offer.

It was one thing to challenge David to finally "leave his mommy," trust in the Lord, take stock in himself, and venture out of the familiar world of numbness and blackouts and into the uncertain but wondrous enterprise of life. But it was quite another thing to encourage his mother to stay on the sidelines as David endured the inevitable bruises of battle from the ordeal that would eventually strengthen and sustain him. I sometimes joked with Martha that I might have to tie her to a chair if she couldn't make herself stand by while her son subjected himself to his custom-designed character-building ordeal. At first, she only pretended to find the comment amusing. But in the end, Martha not only recognized the spirit behind the comment but also came to appreciate both the love and the wisdom inherent in the ordeal with which both she and David had been saddled.

Martha eventually admitted she'd lost faith in God many years before the problems with David began. When her husband was taken from her and David so early, she at first felt betrayed by God. She later came to view God as simply indifferent to her plight. She eventually lost faith in God completely and stopped practicing her religion. It wasn't long after leaving her church that she began losing faith in David as well. And with each personal failure on his part, she lost even more faith in him. About the only thing she continued to believe in through the years was her love for him, and she simply couldn't bear the thought that further harm might come to him or that she might lose him. These were the forces driving her excessive investment in David's welfare: fearing that she might once again lose what she held so dearly, and having trust only in the unwavering love she had for her child.

At first, Martha was very hesitant to even entertain the notion that the ordeals conferred upon David might be *exactly* what he needed to come to better terms with his deficiencies of character and overcome the impediments to a better relationship with the Almighty. She just didn't have that much faith in him. But it would also become apparent that Martha didn't actually believe all that much in herself either. She only believed in the strength of the affection she felt for David. She knew what she was capable of when it came to looking out for his welfare. Demonstrating her abundant concern was one of the few things that made her feel powerful. But other than that, she had little faith in herself. The classic dynamics of codependence were painfully clear: David needed his mother to bend over backward for him to feel any sense of worth, and his mother needed to demonstrate the strength of her devotion to feel any sense of personal power. Clearly, need, not love, was the energy behind this family's dysfunctional dance.

Martha actually had a tougher time in therapy than did David in coming to terms with the ultimate realities of life. In her heart of hearts, she had always wanted a heaven on earth for herself as well as for her family. So when her idyllic dream crumbled so early on, she felt quite betrayed. Even during her churchgoing years, she never embraced the notion that the "way of the cross" is *the* way, the *only* way, for *all* of us. And the unrealistic expectations she held led her to lose faith fairly easily when disappointments came. This was especially true when she lost her husband. Her inability to embrace hardship also led her to fear becoming involved in a new relationship as well as to overprotect her son. Martha didn't see (as Scott Peck points out in *The Road Less Traveled*, 15) that once we make the decision to accept the hardships of life, the entire burden becomes lighter. And she never really appreciated what Christ had to say about the yoke and burden of a life rooted in that faith (Matthew 11:30). But she eventually came to realize that there simply is no life without risk and trial, and that her earlier fantasy about a heaven on earth had actually done a lot to devastate her spirit.

Martha and David eventually came to recognize how unhealthily they had leaned on (and unwittingly used, exploited, and abused) each other to avoid the distinctly personal tasks of reckoning with their disappointments and coming to terms with the deficiencies of their faith. In the process, however, they began recognizing their numerous blessings, facing the inescapable uncertainties of life, and concomitantly, intimately reengaging with and learning to trust in their God. Slowly, they exorcised from their hearts the feeling that they'd been cheated and recovered a sense of gratitude for their lives. And as David's sense of gratitude grew and deepened, he reclaimed a sense of obligation, especially the obligation to keep himself healthy and sober, and to do something meaningful with the life and the talents he'd been given by his God.

This case really exemplifies how hard it is to be grateful sometimes. And the number of problems that can arise out of our ingratitude is quite remarkable. The problem is actually as old as humankind. You can even see it in the story of Adam and Eve in the garden. When contemplating the Eden myth, most Christian scholars and thinkers have traditionally emphasized the disobedience aspect of our first parents' fateful transgression. As the story goes, and as so many have interpreted it, God cautioned both of them not to do something, but they did it anyway and both they and all humanity paid a dear price for their distinctive act of defiance. But little attention is given to what could have made them vulnerable to such a temptation in the first place. Yes, they were given free will, so they had the power to disobey. And, of course, they did defy. But what would make them want to do so? They were literally living in a paradise. They already had everything (although one could argue they didn't sufficiently appreciate that fact). Still, they were somehow lured into challenging the wishes of the very One who had not only granted them life but also given them all they needed to live it happily.

The serpent convinced Adam and Eve that they were cheated by a jealous Creator who didn't want them to have something he knew to be even more valuable (the awareness of things good and bad) than all they'd already been given. This is how they were so effectively seduced. Their vanity did them in. They bought the tempter's lie that they could be like God. When you think about it, it was really pride, the father of all sins (Thomas Aquinas), which made them succumb to temptation and abandon their faith in the Lord.

A literal reading of the story also tells us that our first parents were cast out from Eden as a result of their transgression. But as John Sanford points out (*The Kingdom Within*, 70–81; *Mystical Christianity*, 137–39), it's simply impossible for God to rule where vanity already reigns. So the bigger truth revealed in the garden myth is that God's will and human vanity can never occupy the same space, especially in the heart. Looking at it that way, Adam and Eve weren't really driven out of paradise by a jealous and vengeful god. Rather, in their vanity, they locked themselves out of the Divine presence. And that vanity was still very much on display when, instead of accepting responsibility for their actions and the consequences, they started pointing fingers: first Adam at Eve, then Eve at the serpent and his power of deception. In my many years of working with folks struggling with character issues, I've seen more problems arise out of a person's false pride or vanity than just about any other personality defect.

Humility and gratitude are absolutely essential to cultivating a sense of obligation. A lack of humility and gratitude inevitably begets a sense of entitlement and unrealistic expectation. And only when we truly appreciate what the ultimate Gift Giver has blessed us with can we acquire a sense of responsibility to give something back. What we do with the many gifts we are given, and how we value the many blessings bestowed on us is absolutely crucial to our character development. And there's research that shows that gratitude is really good for us in other ways (Emmons and McCullough, *The Psychology of Gratitude*; Emmons, *Thanks! How the Psychology of Gratitude Can Make You Happier*). But in a world of plenty, it's easy for our sense of appreciation to wane and quickly evaporate when trials appear. You can get pretty bitter when you believe you're owed something in the first place and then bad things happen.

When people undergo ordeals of the kind Martha and David experienced, it's inevitable that both their faith and their characters will be tested. Only a blessed few seem to be able to get through such trials (by the grace of God) with no adverse effects, and even fewer approach them with the anticipation of being strengthened in faith and in character. How a person views this wondrous gift of life, with all its uncertainties and challenges, appears to make the difference. And what one feels obliged to do out of gratitude for this precious gift matters even more.

When David reclaimed a sense of gratitude, it was natural for a sense of obligation to follow. He took stock of his talents, stopped feeling sorry for himself and his weaknesses, and became a productive member of society. He even came to a place in his heart where he could not only accept but also actually embrace hardship. He felt vital again. And he had no use for the instant relief from all pain he once found in alcohol and drugs.

When a Person's Concern Is Misplaced

Sometimes a person can act out of genuine concern for another's welfare, but his or her judgment about the nature of the situation is so faulty and the concerns so misplaced, misguided, or misdirected, that he or she does great harm. Even rightly placed concerns can be improperly or problematically expressed. Unfortunately, it's simply not enough to be well-intended.

Christ rightly advised us that before we attempt to remove even a "speck" we think is clouding the vision or judgment of another, we must first be sure that our own vision and judgment aren't distorted, perhaps to an even greater degree (Matthew 7:5; Luke 6:42). The distorted ways we perceive and think about things almost always impair our reasoning and can cause us to misplace or misuse even the best of our concerns. The vignette that follows tells the story of two parents who truly meant well but nonetheless did much more harm than good in their efforts to help their child.

Eric's Story

Tom and Sue had approached me about the possibility of working with their teenage son Eric once before, but I was unable to accommodate them at the time. Now, they were desperate. They were sure the worst was already happening and that drastic intervention would be needed to forestall disaster. Eric was getting into trouble at school and failing some of his courses. He was also flouting all attempts at discipline, finding ways around just about every consequence, continuing to misbehave despite the loss of privileges, and lying about virtually everything. They no longer trusted him and were genuinely worried about where things were headed. Although they couldn't pinpoint why, they were not only afraid *for* Eric but were also becoming afraid *of* him. Would there be no limits to his defiance, they wondered? How bad might things get? At their wits' end, they pleaded with me to at least meet with all of them one time and render an opinion about what needed to be done.

I had already developed a reputation in the professional community for working with individuals with fairly significant disturbances of character. Many of my clients were referred by other professionals who either deemed them non-amenable to the kinds of intervention with which they were familiar, or had simply become exhausted trying to work with them. And in fact, Eric's parents had taken him to two different therapists in the past, without much success. They'd also taken him to a psychiatrist, hoping that medications might succeed where traditional talk therapy had failed. Eric had been diagnosed with a variety of clinical syndromes and tried on several different medications, but nothing seemed to help all that much. Tom and Sue were convinced, based on the pattern of behavior they were witnessing, that Eric was tragically following in the footsteps of his older brother Steve, whose heartbreaking life of deceit, drugs, crime, and all-too-early death continued to haunt them. It was their fervent prayer that there might be something I could do to help them turn things around and spare them the anguish of a similar tragedy with Eric.

The family arrived right on time for the initial two-hour evaluative session. Neither Tom nor Sue struggled for words. They presented a litany of complaints about Eric's behavior, but always expressed what appeared to be genuine concern for his welfare. They lamented that they had taken away almost everything with regard to privileges to no avail. He continued to defy them at every turn. What's worse, he seemed to enjoy the defiance. This was the hardest thing for them to accept. It appeared to them that he relished the pain he was causing them. After all they had done for him, and after all they'd been through, especially with his brother, they wondered how he could be so heartless.

While I was listening to his parents express their concerns, I was also carefully observing Eric's nonverbal behaviors out of the corner of my eye. Although his face did seem to light up a bit when his parents complained about how painful his defiance was to them, he also seemed to sink in his chair and to almost cower whenever they presented a laundry list of his character flaws. Several times, it looked like he wanted to speak, and he would lean forward and start to open his mouth. But he would quickly retreat, appearing to reluctantly, but with a look of resignation, endure what he perceived was an unavoidable ordeal.

The few times that Eric did speak up were quite remarkable. Each time he spoke, he tried to make the case that not only were some of his misbehaviors cast in an overly dramatic and negative light by his parents but also that none of his more sincere attempts at doing well ever garnered much of their attention. They certainly didn't seem to bring much recognition or reward. But Eric did not speak very much. And when he did, most of the assertions he tried to make were quickly eclipsed by the concerns expressed by his parents.

Experience has shown me that there are some critical signs that indicate whether a person is laboring under some degree of what mental health professionals have always called "neurotic" inner conflict as opposed to a serious disturbance of character. Chief among these is whether the designated client feels some sort of internal pressure and motivation to seek help on his or her own versus reluctantly caving in to pressure from others. Other significant indicators are whether the person exhibits signs of anxiety and whether he or she appears genuinely sensitive to issues of guilt and shame. Anxiety, guilt, and shame are the core features of neurosis, whereas the relative absence of these things is a sure indication of character disturbance. And despite the fact that his own parents seemed to think that this young man was seriously disturbed in character, he showed all of these key features of neurosis quite dramatically. My intuition was telling me that he might have been judged quite unfairly by his parents and even by his former therapists. But based on the history I'd been provided, I also wondered whether I might be succumbing to deception myself and underestimating how seriously impaired Eric's character might actually be. So it was both a pleasant surprise and a great relief that once I had a chance to visit with him alone and develop any degree of rapport, he quickly indicated that he wanted to come to see me on his own. And he readily admitted that he knew he had some mental and emotional issues to work on, and that he felt bad because he knew many of the criticisms his parents had voiced about his behavior were true.

Eric acknowledged that he enjoyed thwarting his parents' attempts to control him. He wanted to prove to them that they couldn't just expect him to simply march in lockstep no matter how severely they punished him. He also confessed that he thwarted the attempts of two previous therapists to help matters, in part because he felt they didn't really understand, but more important, because he felt they acted more like agents of his parents' attempted control. He would not let himself be a mere commodity that his parents brought to someone to be "fixed." And he insisted that he didn't really trust them anyway, because they never called him on his antics or correctly pegged them for what they were. Still, he wasn't really happy about the mess he'd made of things, and didn't really understand why he was doing a lot of it. His actions actually made him feel quite bad and he wanted to do differently. But he didn't know how, and he knew he needed help.

Slowly, some things became clear. Eric was not really a bad kid, although he'd been labeled that way by his parents. In fact, he was mostly a lost kid. He had virtually no idea who he was or where he was going. He was trying to find himself and not doing a very good job of it. And he was trying to claim a separate identity from his parents in the most inept way. He didn't really know himself, but he also didn't want anyone else defining him, especially if they were going to define him too harshly and unfairly.

There were some good reasons for Eric to feel so lost. His dad was largely absent as a role model, frequently overly immersed in his work, and only intervening in Eric's life to mete out discipline in the form of harsh punishment whenever Sue had thrown up her hands. For many years, his only real role model was his older brother, with whom he had a sort of love-hate relationship. He loved his brother not only because of the natural bond between them but also because from his earliest days, he looked to his brother as a life guide. But when Steve got on the path of self-deception, self-indulgence, and eventually, self-destruction, Eric felt deeply betrayed.

Eric desperately wanted to be like somebody he could admire. But he couldn't bring himself to be like his brother, who betrayed and deserted him, or his father, who never seemed to want to have much to do with him. He also wanted to feel accepted by his mother. But he didn't want to be smothered or dominated by her. He had only a vague idea of who and what he really was at the core. And he didn't really have much of a guidance system available to him. He was raised in his mother's faith, but he hadn't yet claimed his own faith. He had some sense of his values and goals, but lacked confidence that coming to more deeply know and take ownership of them would make him the kind of person anyone could really love and respect. In truth, he had been hiding from himself for years. His only solid sense of identity came from knowing that he was quite intelligent and had the capacity to give his parents considerable grief. Doing that gave him some sense of power and separateness. Inwardly, he was afraid that who he really was could never possibly be good enough for them or anyone else. He had never received much in the way of validation or encouragement from anyone, especially his parents.

It was very hard for Eric's parents to be patient during the four years I worked with him. They wanted immediate results and whenever things seemed too slow going, they expressed doubts about whether I was on target in my assessment. They thought about routing Eric to yet another therapist several times. Once, Sue told me she thought I'd gone soft in my old age and forgotten my own principles about how to deal effectively with folks with severe character deficiencies. But as time and circumstances would eventually reveal, the real issue with Tom and Sue was not their lack of confidence in me, but their own deeper crisis of faith.

Tom and Sue had been at odds with God ever since Steve died. They tried so hard to understand the ordeal Steve had put them through. They sacrificed much. But in the end, all their efforts proved to be of no avail. They were still paying on Steve's substantial debts and many wounds were still wide open. They simply couldn't understand how God could do such a thing to them. God not only let Steve die but also turned a blind eye to their many prayers and lengthy suffering. Believing that God simply didn't care, convinced that things were solely up to them, and determined not to allow what happened to Steve to happen again with Eric, they took quick action when they saw him develop disturbing behaviors. Nipping things in the bud was the best chance, they thought, to save their son as well as their own sanity. And they were cautiously hoping that therapy for Eric might possibly save them another heartbreak.

Time would prove Eric to have not only the strongest faith among his family but also the most inspiring and remarkable relationship with his God. He couldn't quote the Bible like his parents, and he not only seemed ignorant of but also took issue with several of the precepts of his church. He couldn't even express his understanding of God as easily as his pastor or his parents seemed to do. But in the pit of his soul, he was deeply aware of God's existence and definitely had a space for God in his heart. He talked openly about the various issues he had with God, and in the process of sharing he made clear to the both of us his values and most ardent beliefs. He believed in honesty, even if that meant acknowledging his numerous sins (which he did in my presence many times). He was also honest about his deep ambivalence about many crucial religious matters—even the very nature of God. But he believed in love, knowing not only that he wanted and desperately needed it but also that he wanted to give it away as purely and freely as possible. He just didn't know how. He'd never been shown the way. Every time he tried to reveal some of his spirit, no one seemed to notice or appreciate it. And every time he took a wrong turn, he not only got noticed but also was slammed for it. He also felt condemned in character for even considering the inappropriate path. He never felt guided toward a better direction, and he didn't trust his own inner voice. It would be my job to challenge him constantly to be faithful, not necessarily to the precepts of his religious denomination, or even to his parents' expectations, but to the beautiful Voice inside of him ready to love and lead him.

Eric eventually stopped fighting with his parents as he began honoring the principles of honesty and love he'd always harbored in his heart but was too angry and wounded to display. He also forgave his parents for much of the pain he felt they caused him. There was little doubt in his mind that they loved him, even though they had horribly misjudged him. He knew they were well-intentioned for the most part, and he also knew he hadn't done much to help them see things more accurately. He would have to forgive himself for this. And his forgiveness of his parents would help them forgive themselves.

Eric also admitted that he'd been fooling himself for some time about a lot of things. His acknowledgment of this fact paved the way for him to gain the insights he really needed to make meaningful changes in his life. He came to realize how poorly adjusted he had been on a social level, and how he'd compensated for that in the past by trying to prove intellectual superiority over others. He also came to recognize that the blanket acceptance he once afforded to others was rooted not so much in a noble or loving nature, as he had often told himself, but rather in his own insecurity and fear of losing the support he desperately craved. He eventually gained the courage not only to confront others when they behaved badly but also to stand firmly on his own principles. Most important, Eric became aware of the real reason for his long history of self-defeating behavior. For years, he'd told himself that he was simply resisting the demands placed on him by others, especially his parents, because he resented their lack of faith in him. He thought he was spitting in the eyes of those he perceived did not appreciate him and from whom he really wanted unconditional positive regard. But the greater truth was that he lacked faith in an unconditionally loving God who not only blessed him with ample gifts but also desired that he use those gifts in the service of his own prosperity as well as the welfare of others. God permitted his brother to be taken from him. But that did not mean that God didn't want him to develop and prosper. For a long time, he feared fully investing himself in anything, always fearing what the Lord might deign to take away. But from now on, he would have both feet in the enterprise of life and he would no longer be his own worst enemy when it came to achieving things.

I'm convinced that a key factor in Eric's therapy success was his acceptance of the notion of merit and the prescriptions I gave him for cultivating a healthy sense of it. Merit is one of those things that many religious denominations inadvertently underplay the value of when emphasizing the role of faith in salvation. Affording oneself appropriate recognition and credit for the always difficult but crucially important task of making the right choice and doing the right thing is the essence of merit and is absolutely essential to developing a healthy sense of self-respect. And I'm not talking here of the false pride or the inflated self-esteem that is the father of sins and can lead to a grandiose sense of self-worth. Moreover, I've always taken care to differentiate between self-esteem and self-respect (Simon, *Character Disturbance*, 87–90). And the two concepts have their roots in different sources. Self-esteem is literally the estimate we make of our self-worth based on our talents and abilities. Self-respect, on the other hand, arises out of our reflections upon what we have willed ourselves to do with what we've been given. Folks with inflated self-esteem overly value and falsely claim credit for the things God (or nature, if you prefer) conferred upon them, whereas persons who lack self-respect neither value nor give appropriate recognition to the efforts they make. That's why when I forced Eric to spend at least ten minutes of every session reflecting on his uniquely human capacity—the ability to freely choose—and to recount even the smallest instances when in the face of temptation to do otherwise, he made the more noble choice, everything began to change.

It would be incorrect to say that Eric completely found himself as a result of his work with me. That's because he knows the task of discovering, defining, and faithfully embracing his core beliefs to be an ongoing effort. But during the time I spent with him, I found little reason to doubt how committed he was to that undertaking. He is now fulfilling his mission to use his organizational and managerial skills with a foundation that promotes social justice around the globe.

I recently had a chance encounter with Eric's parents at a benefit dinner for one of our church's charitable endeavors. They were beaming with pride about how well he was doing and expressed much gratitude for all I did for him. But the truth be told, when basically decent people are tormented by unconscious emotional conflicts and act in unhealthy ways as a result, a therapist doesn't have to do very much at all. Afford the troubled person a safe place to vent, set an atmosphere of positivity and acceptance, and display the courage and commitment to be always truthful, and he or she will blossom on his or her own. That's because underneath it all, that person is not happy and has his or her own motivation to change things. He or she just needs to be in an atmosphere where it feels safe and rewarding to do so.

Eric's mother pulled me aside at the dinner to tell me how unbelievable it was that Tom and Eric had grown so close of late. Eric was always calling Tom, looking for guidance on various matters. And Tom, who had confessed to Sue that losing Steve probably had a lot to do with him burying himself in his work for so many years and keeping his distance from Eric, appeared infused with new life as the result of the growing bond between him and his only remaining son.

These days, whenever I see Eric, I'm filled with good feelings. But that's not so much because I credit myself for his turnaround and growing success but rather because Eric is another living witness to the power of the Spirit to transform. Being a witness to that power and the growing solidity of Eric's faith has helped strengthen my own. I'm absolutely convinced that when things go well in that most intimate of encounters we call "therapy," something much bigger than me is at work. And often, all we really have to do is to clear our hearts and minds of disabling attitudes and preconceptions, open ourselves up, and let the Spirit heal and transform.

When Someone Is Generous to a Fault

Sometimes a person can simply be too generous. Giving willingly and freely can no doubt be a virtuous endeavor. But when people give so much of themselves that they not only neglect themselves but also discourage others to do for themselves, it can create significant problems.

The Story of Hilda, Mary, and Henry

Hilda was taken aback when she heard the news. Although her father, Henry, certainly wasn't getting any younger and hadn't been in the best of health lately, it was still a shock to learn he'd suffered a stroke and was now partially paralyzed. Now, she was faced with a real problem: Henry had no wife, and his only sibling had recently passed away. He would need someone looking after him, and she was all the family he had left, being his only child. Hilda's relationship with Henry had been somewhat strained over the years. But he was still her father, and now he really needed her. She couldn't see simply shipping him off to a convalescent facility. Besides, it really wasn't time yet to take such a drastic action. Still, she had some very mixed feelings and reservations about the situation she faced.

Hilda wondered if there could possibly be a worse time in her life to be confronting the issues now before her. She had only recently begun to carve out a decent life for herself. For years, she'd been taking care of so many others that she had neglected herself in the process. She had been eating poorly, exercising little, and generally not paying much attention to her own welfare. Her weight had become a significant problem, and a lot of the other things she struggled with—the back strain, the knee pain, the high blood sugar and borderline diabetes—were all related to that issue. For too long, eating was one of the few indulgences in Hilda's life, and inasmuch as she denied herself on so many other fronts, it was hard for her to resist that late-night snack or extra piece of pie. But all that had finally begun to change several months ago when she committed herself to an entirely new path. She signed a contract with a fitness center and had started working out every day. She was also watching her sweets, simple carbs, and fats. She was actually starting to pay more attention to herself in general, especially because Mary, her forty-one-year-old daughter, who had moved back in with her on three separate occasions over the past fifteen years, had recently moved out once again, possibly for good. Hilda had finally come to a place where she might possibly claim a life of her own, yet she was once again dealing with the prospect of taking care of someone else. So naturally, she had mixed feelings.

Hilda was also unsure she would even be able to adequately care for Henry. She had few financial resources, and only recently found it possible to cover all the bills with a little left over. She had actually managed to save a bit over the years, and even had some funds set aside a while back for the vacation she'd always wanted to take. But she ended up giving the money to her son so he could buy a new car. He had totaled yet another vehicle and was so upside-down on the note for it that he simply couldn't afford to replace it. She also had to take out an equity loan on her home to help her daughter, Mary, get back on her feet after another failed relationship. She gave Mary enough to go back to school, provided her with a roof over her head at no charge, paid for all the food, and cooked all the meals. Her head was finally above water for the first time in years, but she worried that taking on the care of her father might again drown her in a sea of responsibility and debt.

When Hilda told Mary that she was thinking about taking Henry in, Mary was furious. Mary was finding it way too hard to work part-time, keep up with her classes, and pay the rent on her apartment. So even though she hadn't mentioned it just yet, she was already thinking about moving back in with Hilda. But she knew what might happen if she moved back and her grandfather was also there. Hilda would expect her to pitch in and help with his care. With everything else on her plate, that would be asking far too much. Besides, how could anyone expect her to have a social life and possibly find a new boyfriend if she had to worry about so many other things? It just wasn't fair, and she wondered how Hilda could be so thoughtless.

Hilda asked to see me because she was tormented with guilt. A part of her really wanted to say no to everyone and everything else in her life and say yes to herself for a change. But she also thought that doing so would be a major shirking of her responsibilities as a daughter and mother. This was causing her considerable anxiety and costing her many sleepless nights. It had gotten to the point that she thought about taking those "nerve pills" her family doctor gave her, but she was afraid to do so because she'd been told they were addictive. So I worked her into the schedule as soon as I could.

At first, it appeared like Hilda was primarily seeking some sort of absolution as opposed to guidance. Fortunately, that did not remain the case. Instead of trying to get me to provide her with an acceptable excuse for turning her back on her family and securing permission to tend to her own needs for a change, she actually decided to do some soul-searching about how she might have gotten herself into such a situation in the first place. This was a very good thing, because as caring and well-intentioned a woman as she was, Hilda had very little insight into how she had helped to create the mess that her life had become.

Hilda never missed a session and was always right on time. She worked hard and made good and steady progress. Given the length of time she'd spent ignoring her own concerns and tending to those of others, she had a lot of frustration to get off her chest. So she spent a good deal of time in the first few sessions venting. But gradually she gained some awareness about the root of her problems and started to make some much-needed changes. Her daughter, Mary, could see some of these changes taking place and it was no surprise to me that she became unnerved about this. Mary pressured her mother to allow her to accompany her on a therapy visit to share some of her own thoughts on the situation, and Hilda, not yet being sufficiently healthy, acquiesced to this demand.

When Mary began voicing her concerns, a person might have thought at first that she had her mother's interests in mind. She talked about how difficult it would be for anyone who was not a professional to properly care for her grandfather. And she talked about how tiring it would be for a person her mother's age to tend to his needs twenty-four hours a day. But the real reasons for Mary's concern surfaced fairly quickly. She began complaining about how the rug was about to be pulled out from under her just as she was getting her life together. She also complained that her grandfather was never there for the family and that through the years he and Hilda weren't even on speaking terms half of the time. So she didn't see why Hilda would even consider taking him in. Besides, Mary was busy going to school. And she was trying to have a social life. She just couldn't keep working part-time and would have to give up her apartment. She needed a place to stay but the house simply wasn't big enough for her, Hilda, and her grandfather too. Besides, he would demand lots of Hilda's time and energy. Who would do the cooking? Who would do the cleaning? Who would do the laundry? She had a much better plan: Hilda should declare Grandpa incompetent and get power of attorney. She should put his place on the market, sell off all his assets, and keep the profits. She should then put him in a nursing home that accepted public assistance as full payment. The money could then be put to good use. Mary could pay for school, wouldn't have to worry about working, could focus more on her studies, and could even have a decent social life. She had thought about this a lot. It was the best possible situation for everyone.

If I hadn't heard it firsthand, I probably wouldn't have believed it. And if she were twenty years younger, much of what Mary had said wouldn't have been so shocking. But at forty-one years old, Mary was anything but a mature adult. She was even more self-centered and irresponsible than many teenagers with whom I'd worked. And her relationship with her mother was for the most part parasitic. She was a spoiled little monster. And Hilda, God bless her, had unwittingly helped create this monster.

Hilda actually raised two monsters. It was a classic, unfortunate, but all too common scenario: a parent with enough conscientiousness for an army and children who never had much reason to develop any thoughtfulness of their own. Hilda raised her children as a single mom, as their father deserted the family right after Mary was born. But Hilda was determined to take care of her family and she put every ounce of energy she had into the enterprise. She did everything for her children, and I mean *everything*. She overindulged them both to the point that they had little motivation to grow up, at least on the dimension of personal responsibility. Hilda gave, and they took. That's how it worked— for years. And whenever Hilda tried to take a little bit for herself, they played on her out-of-bounds conscientiousness to manipulate her into denying herself in favor of them. Her brother was good at this, but Mary was much better.

Hilda would gain many powerful insights through her therapy. Her fondest dream had always been to have a family. Her own family had fallen apart just before she entered her teens. But in the early years, it seemed to her that her life was idyllic, and she kept the memories of those years close to her heart. But just as she was entering middle school, her mother suddenly and without warning ran off with another man, never to be heard from again.

Her father became a bitter and resentful person and developed a sour attitude toward all women. He briefly flirted with the idea of remarrying, but all agreed that the woman he was considering would have been the stepmother from hell. By the time Hilda was in high school, she couldn't wait to be out of her father's house and start a family of her own. And she promised herself that she would do things right, and would recapture the feeling she had as a younger child. She dropped out of school, married her high school sweetheart, and within nine months her son was born. Only fourteen months later, she had a baby girl. Barely six months after that, her husband decided he really wasn't ready for such a commitment and left. Still, Hilda was determined that she would have her family. She would take care of everything. If everything were taken care of, and if no one were ever unhappy, then no one would leave. Little did Hilda know how painfully her deepest wish would be fulfilled.

Hilda's son would have three failed marriages and would give up two promising careers for the fast life of parties, women, and drugs. He too would move back home from time to time, but he never stayed long because not having a place of his own really cramped his style. Mary, on the other hand, never really left the house. And she never forged a career for herself. Although she didn't complete high school, she did manage to secure a GED. And she made several stabs at a college education, doing multiple stints at a community college, but she just couldn't seem to make herself stay in classes, or devote sufficient time for study. Academic work never seemed to come easily for her, and if she had spent all the time it would have taken to get the grades, she would never have had a social life. And nothing meant more to Mary than having a good social life. She just knew that one of these days she was going to find that charming prince who would sweep her off her feet. He would have the financial resources that would enable her to lead the good life without having to work. She'd almost found him five times before. She'd succeed one of these days, she just knew it.

So this was Hilda's perfect little family. She got at least one thing she'd always wished for: nobody seemed to really leave home. But it was not the family she'd always envisioned. She wasn't even the mother she'd always wanted to be. She was more like a wet nurse being sucked completely dry by ravenous infants who refused to grow up. All she really wanted was for everyone to be happy and content and never go away. And she did everything she could to make that happen. The dream came true, in nightmarish fashion. She had done far too much and for the wrong reasons. And now that she was facing the prospect of having to do more—this time for a really good reason—she was depleted in energy and spirit.

Matters of faith also factored heavily in Hilda's situation. For many years, Hilda felt betrayed by God and her former church. Her parents had been very active churchgoers and Hilda was very fond of her congregation. All her friends attended the various youth ministry activities and every summer they all went to vacation Bible school together. She saw her life and her family not only as perfect but as God's loving gift to her. When it all fell apart, she felt completely betrayed. And when the parents of two of her closest friends divorced shortly after her own life fell apart, she began questioning everything. Church was a sham, and if God was real, God couldn't possibly be so heartless or sadistic as to crush a little girl's spirit as hers had been. Hilda had lost faith completely. She had no faith in God, and especially not in any church. Believing in that kind of stuff is pure fantasy and only brings heartache. If you want a family, you have to pay for it. You have to pay, and pay, and pay. And that's just what Hilda did. She didn't know it, but she had virtually sold her soul for children who would never leave—a bargain she thought would make her happy again, but which only ended up sapping the life out of her.

Interestingly, God intervened and spared Hilda the hardest choice she might have had to make. Her father suffered another, more severe stroke that left him virtually brain dead. And within a few weeks of that event, he was gone. Hilda would not have to face the dilemma of balancing her own interests against the needs of a dependent and disabled parent. But there was still Mary. What would she do?

Hilda worked hard to resolve her issues, despite Mary's best attempts at thwarting her progress. Eventually she came to a place in her heart where she could be comfortable with the notion of being there for her children during a time of genuine need while never again enabling them to not fend for themselves or lead a responsible life. She found the strength to set some very necessary limits with Mary. And she pretty much had to shove her out the door. Mary, of course, went out kicking and screaming. But at least she left standing upright. Hilda's children, both now in their fifties, still haven't fully grown up, although each is making progress. Hilda is not only older but also much wiser now. And she is happy to have the kids come over on holidays. Naturally, they test her from time to time, making clever bids for money and unmerited support. But Hilda holds firm. She wants to enjoy her children, not continue nursing them.

Hilda has come to some very different terms with her faith.

She had been so mad at God for so long because she thought God had betrayed her early in life. But through her ordeal she came to appreciate that God's role in our lives was never meant to be as nursemaid. Yes, God allows things to happen. God also permits us to experience the consequences of our actions. And sometimes, the impact of that can be quite substantial and devastating. But it can also be powerfully instructive, but only if we have faith. Hilda can see that now. God really never betrayed her nor did God desert her. She was betrayed by her own lack of faith, which drove her to indulge others to the point of neglecting herself. And instead of creating the idyllic family she yearned for, she fostered the kind of selfishness in her children that made that kind of family impossible. God, she realized, wishes, just as the great commandment exhorts, that we love others, not more than or less than, but *as* we love ourselves. And loving properly always involves setting and enforcing limits and boundaries. Her faith restored, Hilda respects those boundaries more these days. She actually has more of the family she always wanted. She also has her own home, her own life, and her health. She had always desired these things, and had been working toward them. But for a long time she couldn't say no when she needed to, and thought things would happen by magic. Her daughter, Mary, has the same penchant for magical thinking. But the grace of God and circumstances put Hilda through an ordeal that taught her some invaluable lessons about the real nature of personal responsibility. And because she could eventually view that ordeal as a blessing, she was able to reclaim her faith.

When she stopped to reflect on it all, Hilda wondered how God could possibly have been more faithful. She also wondered how she could have possibly been so blind. Her unrealistic assessment of her early life, her sense of betrayal when it fell apart, and her unconscious determination to make things right in the only way she knew how led her to the brink of self-destruction. She knows that now. But she also believes she never would have come to know it were it not for the events that unfolded shortly after her father fell ill. God had been faithful all along. It was she who broke faith. In a way, her early relationship with her heavenly Father paralleled the relationship her own children had with her for such a long time. When everything she wanted was given her, she was happy. When she felt denied, she also felt betrayed. She and her children would all have to learn some very different things about the nature of love and fidelity. Could God have possibly been more faithful? Could she have been any more blind? Hilda doesn't think so. And she believes that she owes this new perspective to her ordeal and God's loving grace.

WHEN GOOD PEOPLE DON'T DO ENOUGH

There is an old saying, often attributed (though many historians claim, erroneously) to Edmund Burke that "the only thing necessary for the triumph of evil is for good men to do nothing." The saying reflects a deep truth. Evil is like a cancer. It easily infects our lives and spreads without active, intense intervention.

Genuine faith in Christ and his message of love, forgiveness, and righteous living demands more from us than tender sentiments toward others. It demands action. And Christ commanded those who would call themselves his followers to unwaveringly display that love even to the lowliest among us and even when our instincts try to steer us in another direction.

Ardent, righteous loving is not the kind of overstretching of responsibility in which some folks mistakenly engage. That kind of behavior only enables irresponsible individuals to further renege on their social obligations, as I've tried to illustrate through some examples in the previous chapter. But accepting the duty for loving, virtuous conduct is exactly what Christ expects of his followers. He did not command his disciples to simply feel a certain way or say particular things. Rather, he commanded them to *do* in the same manner he modeled throughout his ministry. Testifying to Christ is not so much a matter of proclaiming his name and preaching his works as it is living on an entirely new spiritual plane infused with his grace. Such living can only be made possible by complete faith and trust in the One who gave us such an unnatural instruction.

In the vignettes that follow, I hope to illustrate how evil can prevail simply because basically good and decent people don't do enough to impede it. Sometimes that failure arises out of shaky faith. At other times, it's the result of laziness, indifference, or even fear. Sometimes, especially in families, it happens because someone is more than willing to take up all the slack, so no one else has much motivation to do any work. There are many possible reasons. But in the end, the only way to overcome evil is with righteous action—action prompted by faith in the Christ who commanded us to take it. As the word *righteous* suggests, doing the right thing also means being in right relationship with God.

The Story of Paul, Betty, and John

At least on the surface, the Blake family appeared to enjoy a life most others would envy. Paul and Betty cared for each other and had been together for twenty-five years. John, their pride and joy, was an excellent student and had never been a problem to anyone. Given my reputation in the community for dealing primarily with individuals who had behavioral and character problems, I was naturally curious about why John's mother was asking me to make an appointment for him as soon as possible.

It probably should have been a tip-off to me about where some of the important issues might lie when Betty asked the seemingly bright, handsome, and genteel young man of twenty to remain seated in the waiting room while she spoke with me alone at first. I was a bit hesitant about this but John readily assented. Betty was quick to downplay the notion that John was having any major problems. Still, she thought it might be good for him to see someone, and a friend had given her my name. But before providing me with any more background, Betty stated that one of the main reasons she made the appointment and the reason she'd asked to speak with me first was that she needed a written statement from a professional making the case to officials at John's college that he simply could not handle the stress of being placed in a two-person dorm room. The school needed this documentation soon, which is why she needed the appointment quickly. She implied that writing the letter was a mere formality, and that a prior therapist had done this very same thing for her the semester before, having agreed with her that John was an especially sensitive child who becomes stressed out easily and simply didn't need to be subjected to the infantile antics of a typical college roommate. The college acquiesced to this request but wanted to make a change for the coming semester. The nature of Betty's request and her relative silence on other matters was a much bigger red flag about what might be amiss, as was the fact that John had already been to another therapist. And the fact that Betty was taking such a dominant role in the whole process also seemed a bit curious. So while it took some doing, I politely but deftly sidestepped responding to Betty's request for the letter until I'd had a chance to visit with John a few times to complete a proper evaluation of circumstances.

From the outset, the time I spent with John individually was quite remarkable. The thing that impressed me most about him was how intelligent, thoughtful, and extremely well-mannered a young man he seemed to be. His manner of interacting was certainly not that of a typical college sophomore. And despite his somewhat reserved demeanor, he seemed relatively open to sharing information, even though we were meeting for the first time.

John asked what his mother might have told me about him and whether she had already asked for a letter for him to secure a private dorm room. I asked him whether he shared his mother's view that having a private room was a necessity, and he merely shrugged his shoulders and displayed an air of indifference. So I invited John to simply begin telling me about himself and any concerns that he might have.

John seemed to feel obliged to talk first about what had been going on with him lately that he surmised might have prompted his mother to nudge him into seeing someone. It seems that toward the end of the last semester, he had been increasingly skipping class and hanging out with a few of the more unmotivated crowd on campus. He also began finding himself using increasing amounts of marijuana. His grades took a bit of a hit as a result. None of these behaviors alone was all that atypical from those of other college-age clients I'd counseled. But John readily acknowledged that they were quite out of character for him. He had always been an outstanding student and never shirked his responsibilities. So he understood why his mother might have been concerned. I did my best to create an atmosphere in which John could feel free to muse about what issues might be underlying his recent atypical behavior when he dropped a real bombshell. He said he'd been feeling fairly down for quite a while and even had the thought cross his mind once or twice that maybe he'd be better off if he weren't alive.

During the next several visits I had with John, it became abundantly clear that he was in much deeper psychological pain than showed on the surface. It became evident that John had a weak sense of personal identity and a poorer sense of direction or purpose in life than most young persons his age. He had been socially removed for quite some time, even during most of his high school days. And he spent most of his first semester at college holed up in his private room studying. Only recently had he begun coming out of his shell. His social isolation, feelings of emptiness, and many of the other things he reported all pointed in one direction: he was significantly depressed. This fact stood in stark contrast to his mother's characterization of things during the first visit.

John talked a lot about his mother. He was in a real bind with respect to the relationship he had with her. He loved her immensely and knew that she loved him. And she was virtually his only confidant. He was probably closer to her than anyone else on earth. But she could nearly smother him with her care and concern. And because for years she had doted upon him, coddled him, and overly protected him, he never learned how to do very much for himself. As a result, he felt weak, ineffectual, and more than a little worthless.

John admitted that he hadn't invested much energy in his prior brief therapy experience. He didn't get the feeling his former therapist was all that interested in him or even concerned about him, especially given how much time he seemed to spend talking to his mother and responding to her expressed wishes and concerns. And his mother didn't press the issue of him remaining in treatment, especially after she secured the letter she wanted the therapist to write.

John talked quite a bit about how weak and unmotivated he felt. He didn't really think he was gay (he felt attracted to women and was revolted by even the thought of being with a man) yet he had been questioning his sexual identity for years because he felt so unmanly. And he was so used to his mother's unconditional approval of him that the slightest hint of rejection from any girl was enough to make him run from a relationship that had the potential to become more intimate. Although he had recently found a fairly laissez-faire crowd to associate with, because he had few social skills he kept to himself a lot and had no really close relationships. Much of the time, he felt lonely, misunderstood, anxious, fragile, insecure, ineffective, and, most especially, unhappy.

Conspicuously missing from our earliest conversations was any mention of John's father. The few times that I asked about him directly, John talked very kindly of Paul. He noted that his father was a good man, respected by his family and friends and highly regarded at his work. And John was proud of his father for all the things he had accomplished. But what became abundantly clear as information came pouring in was that Paul had been a strikingly absent presence in John's life.

When John was a young child, Paul was just building his business. He started with nothing but high hopes, a little money he obtained by selling a new car his parents had given him, and making do with a barely running used model he'd kept since high school. He worked very long, hard hours for many years, and his fledgling business frequently teetered on the brink of collapse. In the earliest years, he always remembered to come into the room at night and kiss his young son on the forehead. And he tried to clear as much space as he could on weekends for some family time. But as the demands of his business grew, it seemed that both the time and energy for anything else slipped away. For most things related to family life, especially things involving John, Paul simply wasn't there. He wasn't there for T-ball games or Boy Scouts. He wasn't there for parents' night at school. He wasn't there to pitch a few balls in the back yard. And over the years, it was Betty who always took up the slack. Paul no doubt had affection for John, but Paul simply wasn't there to guide John.

I could see that John was more than a bit nervous when I suggested it might be a good idea for his father, me, and him to meet together. It was quite remarkable how protective he seemed to be of his father. He believed that his father's willingness to work so hard for his family was an undeniable sign of how much he loved them all. He didn't want his father to get the wrong idea about being brought into the therapy process. And even as nervous as John was most of the time, it was clear that just the thought of his father being together with him in such an intimate situation as a therapy session was prompting him to be even more apprehensive.

Paul came across as a decent man who cared very much about his family. He had always been faithful to Betty and never indulged himself with the money he made once his business became successful. He was in church every Sunday and supported many of his congregation's charitable enterprises. There was a lot to admire about Paul.

John appeared almost embarrassed at having his father with him in a therapist's office. The last thing he wanted to do was to bring shame upon or hurt this man he loved. It took all the courage he had to address his concerns, but somehow he found the words necessary to confront his father on the issues that had been needing attention for years. John never chided his father or showed any sign of disrespect. He couldn't even bring himself to express anger toward Paul. Instead, he focused on how much he missed his father and how desperately he needed him to be a bigger part of his life. John poured his heart out to Paul. And Paul, to his credit, was more than receptive. At the end of the hour, John commented that he'd never seen his father cry before that day. He also said that he'd never experienced an embrace from him like the one they shared at the end of the session.

John and Paul had several more sessions together. In the process, they came to realize how much they shared in common. Paul too had always felt he had something to prove with respect to his capabilities and manhood. As is often the case, he also had an impoverished relationship with his own father when he was growing up. And with his lacking confidence in himself as well as a model to go by, he approached his role as father to John with great trepidation. He was not only fearful when it came to engaging with John but also quite jealous of him. Right from the beginning, John seemed to have it all: high intelligence, great looks, and an award-winning smile and personality. On top of all that, he was the apple of his mother's eye. Paul hated to admit it, but he felt he simply couldn't compete and he was determined to prove to everyone—his father, his wife, and especially himself—that he was worthy of their regard. And he thought that the success he was creating for himself in his business would finally demonstrate his worthiness.

As all the issues became exposed, it became evident that Paul also feared John would forever fault him for his failures as a father. It was a monumental insight for Paul and a pivotal point in his relationship with his son when he finally realized how eager John was to accept him just as he was. John didn't want perfection from him. He never did. He didn't even want his approval all that much. What he really wanted more than anything else was *him.* He yearned for the relationship he'd never had. He wanted to talk to, share with, learn from, and yes, to some degree even model after this man he'd long admired from such a distance but from whom he felt so regretfully estranged.

Paul's sessions with his son helped him realize that he also had to do some serious reckoning with the nature of his faith. He went to church, donated faithfully, and did what was required of him because he always wanted to do the right thing. But he realized that he'd never fully embraced the Lord's admonition to relegate concerns about material safety, security, and his personal success to the back burner and instead vigorously pursue the glorification of God through service to God's creation. Instead of putting his love into action (especially with his family and most especially with his son), he was pouring his energy into other endeavors he thought would merit him love and respect. And he did not have the faith—either in himself or in the Lord's exhortation to love and trust above all else—to embrace the notion that rightly directing his heart would be sufficient to bring everything of real value to himself and his family.

John now has a family of his own, and he is not only a loving but also a very involved father. His relationship with Paul gets stronger all the time, just as both his and his father's relationship with the Lord continues to blossom. In finding their faith, these one-time strangers found each other. And in really getting to know each other, they came to a better understanding of themselves and their God. The growth in their relationship parallels the growth they've both experienced as men, husbands, and fathers. In connecting more intimately with the Source of all strength, they have both found their own strength—a strength rooted in faith and expressed without shame in a most wholesome and endearing love.

The Story of Ellen and Marci

Ellen had been married to Ed a little more than a few months when she noticed things beginning to change with her daughter, Marci. Ellen's first husband, Frank, had left her for a much younger woman almost seven years ago. And over the past few years, Frank had much less contact with Marci than he did at first. Marci and Frank seemed to be so close in Marci's younger years. So Ellen sometimes wondered if the change in Marci's behavior was in some way related to her feelings about the growing distance between her and her father.

Ellen thought she'd never recover from the betrayal of trust and the wound of learning that Frank had actually been unfaithful to her for many years—even during their honeymoon! And although she had some concerns about Ed, at least he seemed the caring sort. He was also a good provider. And he appeared to take to Marci from the outset of their relationship, even doting on her at times. So it struck Ellen as a bit odd that Marci never seemed very appreciative of Ed and frequently expressed her dislike of him. But she figured this had less to do with Ed and much more to do with Marci's estrangement from Frank. She surmised that given how close Marci was to Frank in the early years of her life, she might be more than a little hesitant to let a new father figure into her life.

Marci was not only having a tough time adjusting to Ed but was also doing some things lately that appeared quite out of character. And she was doing these things more and more often. Marci was increasingly argumentative and defiant. Ellen thought this might simply be normal adolescent rebellion. But she was doing other things that were cause for concern too. Marci had been caught many times being untruthful, especially when questioned about her activities outside the home. And lately she'd been spending much more time away from the house and with her friends. Her grades at school had slipped fairly significantly, largely because of how much time Marci was away and how little time she spent at home doing homework. Ellen's grounding Marci was becoming a much more regular occurrence.

Ellen's relationship with Marci was becoming uncharacteristically strained and distant. Ellen felt like Marci might be angry with her but couldn't fathom a reason why. And Marci rarely even spoke to Ed. Even though he was always the one to intervene and push for leniency whenever Ellen grounded Marci, Marci never seemed to appreciate Ed's advocacy on her behalf.

One day, when Ellen was confronting Marci about her apparent ingratitude, especially toward Ed, Marci blurted out, "He gives me the creeps!" and stormed off. Sometime later, she complained that she didn't like the way he looked at her most of the time. But the one time Ellen inquired further about this, Marci couldn't come up with anything specific about Ed that seemed inappropriate. So Ellen figured this was just another of Marci's many ways of trying to justify her ever-increasing rebelliousness.

Besides, the more she caught Marci lying about other things, the harder it was for her to take any of her comments seriously, especially when most of the time, whenever she had anything bad to say about Ed or even Ellen, it was when she was in trouble for something.

Marci was about to be grounded again for lying about where she had really been the other evening when she was supposed to be at a girlfriend's house studying, when she blurted out, "What do you care, anyway? You don't care about me or what I want or how I feel. You married one guy who doesn't even care about me anymore and then you went and married a guy who gives me the creeps. He's always making lewd comments to me, and he freaks me out with the way he looks at me. I don't like it when he touches me, either. There's something really nasty about it. And when I tell him to back off he has the nerve to tell me things like he can get me ungrounded and out of trouble if I'll just be more 'friendly' to him. He's the last guy I want to be friendly with! I don't want to even be near the guy! This is the last place on earth I want to be anymore. I'd rather be out with my friends. At least they care. No one here really cares about me or how I feel." And with that, Marci stormed out once again.

Part of Ellen was flabbergasted. Could she really have been so blind for so many months to have not noticed any inappropriate behavior on Ed's part? But another part of her was full of doubt. Marci only seemed to say these kinds of things when she was in trouble. And she'd been caught lying so much of the time and about so many other things recently that it was hard to take what she had to say at face value. Ellen just didn't know what to believe. Still, she thought she'd better confront Ed.

Ellen could almost have anticipated Ed's reaction when she challenged him on whether he'd ever done or said anything inappropriate to Marci. "I bet she was in trouble when she said it, wasn't she?" was his immediate response. "Well, there's your answer," was his follow-up. "You know she lies, and rather than take the heat for her own misbehavior, she starts pointing the finger at me," he insisted. Then, as if Ellen didn't feel bad enough already for having to confront him, Ed added, "You know she's never liked me from day one because for a long time she's had no father to corral her. She's gotten used to having no strong authority in the house. All she wants is to be able to do as she pleases. If you take her side, you'll only be making things worse."

Ellen would remember for the rest of her life the day the truth of the whole sordid mess became apparent. She had come home at an unexpected time and entered her bedroom while Ed happened to be showering. On the bed was his camera, which he usually guarded with his life, and to her great shock, still on the display panel was a snapshot of her daughter, Marci, mostly naked after getting out of the shower. The framing of the photo made it quite apparent that the picture had been snapped by someone peering through a partially opened bathroom door. There were other photos, too—equally appalling. Ellen suddenly felt sick to her stomach. Marci had been telling the truth all along, and she really hadn't been listening carefully enough nor doing enough to protect her.

It took some doing, but Ellen managed to convince Marci to come to a counseling session with her. They both approached the prospect of reconciliation with a great deal of apprehension and trepidation. At some level, both wanted to mend their deeply fractured relationship. But it was also abundantly clear that each of them was suffering some deep crisis of faith. It would be hard for them to have faith in the process that characterizes good therapy because sometimes that very process is itself quite painful. It was necessary to be acutely mindful of their weakness of faith through much of the first phases of treatment.

As Marci and Ellen worked through their issues, it became clear that they both had lost faith in many things. Their crisis of faith had actually begun some time ago, after they had been so deeply wounded by Frank. Over time, they had come to lose faith in themselves, in each other, and in their God.

Marci first lost faith in some of the principles her parents had always advocated. Marital fidelity seemed like more of a myth or even a joke to her. And as if it wasn't enough to lose faith in her own father when he proved himself so untrustworthy, after her experience with Ed, she had come to mistrust all men. Her confidence in her religion as well as her faith in God was deeply shaken because they had both allowed her world to fall apart. But because they had once been so close, perhaps the most uniquely painful thing for Marci to bear was the loss of faith in her mother. Marci came to a point where she truly believed there was simply no one who could be trusted. No one could ever really protect her, so she had to start looking out for herself. And believing she couldn't count on anyone else's guidance, she felt she had to chart her own course. Feeling this way, she had retreated into a lonely, desperate, and depressing place, and couldn't find a reason to trust anything or anyone else to bring her out. This was most unfortunate because at some level she knew that she still needed guidance and direction more than anything. So despite the fact that a large part of her wanted to, the thought of reconciling with her mother caused her pangs of deep ambivalence.

Ellen had lost faith too. She lost faith in her religion after her pastor, who repeatedly counseled her to do her best to keep her marriage with Frank together, proved himself to be just as unfaithful to his own wife as Frank had been to her. She lost faith in her daughter, to whom she had been so close and admired for many years but who appeared to have turned into someone she hardly knew anymore. And she eventually had her faith in God shaken because God had seemed to have stood by idly while her life collapsed right before her eyes, not once, but twice! And most especially, she lost faith in herself. She wondered how unattractive she must really be for a man to cheat on her after only a few days of marriage and to eventually dump her for what he openly boasted was a younger and more attractive model. She had also come to question the soundness of her judgment. Feeling a failure, and coming to the opinion that there must be something about her that decent men found unattractive, she "settled" for Ed—the best she thought she could get at the time. And when doubts arose about him, she cast them aside out of fear that she'd lose the little stability and security she'd managed to obtain in her life. Frank had left her both penniless and brokenhearted. She did her best to fend for herself and Marci but she just couldn't make it until Ed came around. Things with him were never perfect, but at least she and Marci had a decent roof over their heads. A part of her knew that if there was even a chance that what Marci had been telling her early on was true, she should have been prepared to pack up and move out. But her fears got the best of her, and she simply couldn't allow herself to believe it. And now she could only blame herself for a mess bigger than she could have ever anticipated—all because of her lack of faith.

In therapy, Ellen came to realize that in addition to being negligent with Marci, she had actually been negligent about her own welfare, and for quite some time. She realized that there were plenty of red flags about Ed, even before she married him. But she put the blinders on because she didn't trust herself or her instincts, and she didn't know if she could make it in life on her own. It took quite a lot for Ellen to eventually forgive herself.

Marci eventually came to realize the problems caused by her failure to take more direct action to address the issues that had been concerning her regarding Ed. At the time she was going through the ordeal with Ed, however, she was not in an emotionally trusting place. Not trusting her mother's judgment, not knowing what to do herself, and not having much faith in God, she tried to handle things by herself and in her own, now admittedly immature, way. Gaining awareness into this really helped Marci make peace with and forgive her mother.

Marci and Ellen's forgiveness of each other was actually the first and most essential step in the process of forgiving themselves. In that same process, they also slowly recovered their faith. They regained faith in themselves, faith in each other, and faith in the love that ultimately saved them. They'd heard it said many times before: God is love. But now they had a deeper level of understanding. They were able to see something in this most profound and divine equation that they'd never really realized before at any meaningful level. Yes, God is Love. That necessarily means that love—pure, right-spirited, boundless love—is God! And while none of us can ever achieve the level of love that is the Lord, we can put our trust in Love. Love can truly save us. Love can rescue us from the very pit of despair. In their days of impoverished faith, both Marci and Ellen settled for a lot of things as a substitute for the love they really wanted but felt unworthy of possessing. But renewed in faith, and more keenly aware of the unconditional nature of God's regard for them, they would never again settle for anything less than real love.

WHEN DECENT PEOPLE FAIL THE CHARACTER TEST

All of us have our shortcomings and deficiencies of character. And it's when adversity or temptation tests our character that our faults become exposed. When we remain ever mindful of our weaknesses, do our best to honestly reckon with them, and take deliberate care to nurture our faith, we're not as likely to get ourselves into trouble when difficult circumstances arise. But it's simply too easy, even for basically decent and God-fearing folks, to go through life with a dangerous degree of inattentiveness to our inner lives. Bad things usually happen when we haven't sufficiently tended to our character flaws and lack the solidity and strength of faith to pass safely through times of trial.

Becky's Story

Becky was used to taking the backseat. For as long as she'd known him, Randy always seemed to command center stage.

And he had the energy, the personal charisma, the quick wit, and, above all, the confidence to be the undisputed leader of the family. Becky actually blamed herself for not liking him very much anymore. That's because everyone else seemed not only to like him but sometimes even to fawn over him. He seemed such a friendly, outgoing, and engaging guy, and was the life of every party. In fact, that's one of the main reasons she was drawn to him in the beginning. But as time went on, she felt she was under Randy's shadow most of the time, and she didn't like that feeling at all. She also didn't like the fact that things always seemed to go Randy's way, even when she sincerely thought they shouldn't. He never consulted with her, even on the big decisions. There was the time he went out and bought a new boat for himself that they could barely afford, and the time he traded in a still very low-mileage family car just because a new sports model had caught his eye. He seemed to act without hesitation when it came to something he wanted for himself, and showed surprisingly little regard for how his decisions might negatively affect anyone else. And it seemed pointless to bring concerns to his attention because he always had answers ready that at least on the surface appeared reasonable. In the end, Randy always managed to get just what he wanted. Yet it was like pulling teeth to get him to pay attention to things she or the kids really needed. Randy always seemed to expect everyone else to accede to his wishes. And Becky was sure he took her fidelity for granted.

The one place where Becky felt truly recognized or appreciated in any way was at her church's small charitable foundation. She worked part-time managing the schedules of several of the most active social ministries and doing light bookkeeping. Becky felt good when she was there. People were always saying things like they didn't know what they'd do without her and how easy it was to work with her. But in addition to feeling important, her workplace was the only environment in which she felt she had control over anything—especially over money. She recorded donations, made bank deposits, turned in reports, and made sure that the pastor had an orderly accounting of bills that needed to be paid. Becky loved her job. Work was the one place in her life where she felt her abilities were noticed. She felt capable there and she liked that feeling very much. And she liked the feeling of being in charge of something even more.

Becky always meant to repay the small amounts of cash she occasionally "borrowed" from the petty cash fund. She knew in her heart she wasn't trying to hurt anyone or even to indulge herself. She only used the money for things she and the kids needed. Having to haggle with Randy for every little thing was always so distasteful and demeaning. Whether it was a new pair of khakis for her son Jeff, or some contact lenses so she could see well enough to do her work, Randy made her feel so ashamed for even asking, and berated her for financial ineptness whenever she said she needed any money. She just hated to face him about these things. And she fully intended to pay every cent back. The fact that she hadn't done so just yet did bother her. But she felt that because the amounts she took were so small, the church surely wouldn't suffer in any significant way because of her actions.

Becky was as surprised as anyone when it came to light just how much money was missing. And she bristled when she heard the tax accountant use the word *stolen*. She never thought of herself as a thief. It was hard for her to imagine that the minuscule loans she'd advanced herself over the years added up to several thousand dollars.

Facing the reality of her situation was quite daunting. Becky had no savings of her own and couldn't possibly pay the money back without Randy's help. Facing him would be the most difficult thing she could imagine. It would be asking a lot of Randy to help her out of the trouble she had caused by herself. He would not only have to stick by her, but would have to be willing to deny himself for quite some time so there would be enough money for restitution. She could almost anticipate the look on his face and she simply dreaded the thought of telling him.

As soon as he learned the details of the situation, Randy cleaned out the bank accounts, filed for divorce, and moved out of the house. He smugly told Becky that he had never signed on to the kind of mess she'd made out of things and that she was now totally on her own. He didn't take the boys with him. After all, the swank new apartment he'd found in a trendy section of town was simply too small to accommodate children. Besides, his little sports car wasn't big enough to tote them around in. Becky had the SUV and handling the kids was always her department anyway. Naturally, the kids could visit from time to time, but staying there, even overnight, would be a problem. And Randy made it clear he would not be in the business of bailing Becky out of the trouble she'd caused. He had his attorney already working on a settlement he felt confident Becky would have to accept, and it included only a modest amount for child support.

Becky pleaded guilty to the theft, and was fined, placed on probation, urged to seek counseling, and ordered to make restitution. The court's judgment allowed her to satisfy her debt in installments, but gave Becky little breathing room. Thus began a significant personal ordeal that was to prove pivotal for her character development. She would spend four years in fairly intensive counseling and would work overtime to put enough aside to pay back all that she owed.

During her years of counseling and reflection, Becky gained greater awareness of and came to terms with some key things about herself that she later realized were instrumental in her getting into so much trouble in the first place. She would have to reckon with not only the defects in her character but also the shortcomings of her faith that made her so vulnerable to the temptation to which she had succumbed. During her course of therapy, Becky had to admit some not so pleasant things about herself. She had to acknowledge that she had a very high level of personal ambition. In fact, it's one of the reasons she was so frequently jealous of Randy. She had always wanted to go places in life and to be important. But she also felt unsure of herself. She didn't have the inner confidence that if she put her mind to it and her heart into it, she could achieve whatever she wanted. That's really what made her so hungry for the approval of others and made her want to affiliate with those whom she perceived as more confident. In fact, that's probably the main reason she was drawn to Randy. There never was very much else about him that she found attractive. She realized that now. But he was certainly confident and he almost always seemed to know how to get what he wanted. She gravitated toward him because wherever he was going, she wanted to come along for the ride, even though it didn't take long for her to realize how lonely and demeaning a ride it would be.

Becky also had to admit that she didn't really trust anyone. No one in her family had ever proved to be either a reliable source of support or a sincere advocate. Ever since her teenage years, she had felt pretty much on her own. And she didn't have much trust in God, either. She prayed so hard and so often but God never seemed to hear her. She didn't ask for much. But the windfall she hoped would come her way and free her from the trap she'd made for herself never came. But the hardest thing she had to admit was how little she trusted herself. She wanted so much. Yet she felt she'd never achieve anything of substance because she had no inner sense of confidence. Her tendency to endlessly seek approval and validation was rooted in the fact that she could barely even conceive that anyone else would genuinely consider her worthy. Hers was a life almost devoid of real faith.

Becky had always thought of herself as a Christian. But circumstances made her reflect more deeply than ever about what being a Christian really meant to her. At one time, her identity as a Christian hung on the notion of being accepted into the community of believers. And what was required for entrance to that community was verbally acknowledging before the others that Christ died for our sins and accepting him as personal Savior. But Becky never seriously reflected upon the meaning of Christ's sacrifice or what it should mean for her own life. Nor did she ponder what it really meant to her to be saved. But the ordeal she was presently undergoing made her begin reflecting on such things much more often. And the more she contemplated the meaning of Christ's mission and sacrifice, the more real he became to her. She found herself gradually believing some things she'd never really felt convicted about before. Being a part of Christ's universal church was much more than just being accepted into a group of persons also willing to profess their acceptance of him as Savior. It was about genuinely knowing him, understanding his message to us, and entering into a relationship like none other. No one truly involved in such a relationship could feel about themselves as Becky used to feel about herself. Christ isn't just anyone. He is God in the flesh. And really appreciating how he has saved us goes much deeper than merely acknowledging his redemptive act.

For the first time in her life, Becky was getting to know Christ. As fully human, he completely understood the fears, insecurities, uncertainties, and temptations with which we all struggle. That meant he understood her and what she needed. It also explained why he agonized over the sacrifice he knew he was called to make on our behalf. But he was also divine—the perfect expression of the Father's infinite love for us. And in his love for us he not only imparted to us the words of eternal life (John 6:68) but also provided us the greatest possible manifestation of love and devotion. To sacrifice literally means to make something holy. Christ's death and resurrection were the most holy gifts he could possibly give to us. They are the ultimate signs not only that he literally loves to death but also that we can place our complete faith and trust in him and his message.

Suddenly, Scripture like "Do not worry about your life, what you will eat or what you will drink, or about your body, what you will wear. . . . But strive first for the kingdom of God and his righteousness, and all these things will be given to you" (Matthew 6:25, 33) took on new and powerful meaning for Becky. They weren't simply inspiring words by a charismatic preacher. They were the perfect prescription for the faithless creature she'd always been. She began to feel invited to take the leap of faith she'd always wanted to make but was afraid and felt unworthy to take. And now she was even beginning to believe that the invitation came from none other than the ultimate authority on human needs. For the first time in her life, she began thinking of herself as a person of value. She could now trust the Lord to provide if she would seek God's reign in her life.

Becky's first leaps of faith would change almost everything about her. No longer would she cling to another human being—especially a human being with insufficient regard for her—out of fear that she would fail or perish if she tried to make it on her own. Besides, she was now more aware than ever that she never was and never would be alone. Moreover, she would never again pin her hopes on the material things that she had always lusted after but thought she didn't have the talent or the power to secure. Instead, she would start to put her actions where her verbal professions of faith had always been before. She would place genuine trust in the Lord, and invest herself in righteous living. In the process, she would acquire a quiet and humble confidence she'd never known before.

Becky did not go around proclaiming her newfound faith to everyone she encountered. Rather, she did her best to put that faith into meaningful action each and every day. She tirelessly scoured the area in search of the kind of employment that would not only provide her sufficient income to live modestly, take care of the children, pay off her fines, and make restitution but also enable her to fulfill what she had come to believe was her personal mission on earth. She would search ardently, but mindful of her obligations, she would take whatever reasonable opportunity she could get, at least at first. She wasn't looking for compassion or absolution. She just wanted a chance. Becky eventually found a job at a new, small business doing various clerical tasks. She was upfront with her superiors about her history and made it clear she expected to be well supervised and held accountable. She promised God and herself that she would not only cherish the opportunity she'd been given but also be particularly mindful of any temptations to covet anything that she hadn't truly and honestly earned. Over time, her personable manner and her humble candor became legend around the office. In just a few years she worked her way up to marketing manager and eventually to vice-president in charge of operations. In the process, Becky learned some things she had never known until the ordeal she had to suffer: she could trust the Lord, believe in the Lord's word, and live in accordance with his will, and in so doing would enjoy a greater sense of purpose, fulfillment, and confidence than she had ever known. No longer would she have to endure feeling overshadowed, belittled, or controlled because of how little she thought of herself. She was humbled by the awesome power of faith to transform her life and would be eternally grateful to her God. And although she was more than happy to submit herself to God, she would never again place herself under anyone else's thumb. Feeling inordinately blessed and empowered, she doubted she would ever again feel like she had to surreptitiously take what she knew was within her power to earn. And as Becky gained greater self-assurance, she also began to see God in a new light. As God became less distant, she could also imagine God being pleased and even smiling at her.

The Story of Agnes and Bob

You could ask anyone and they'd tell you that Agnes was the kind of person who would do anything for you. She was also the consummate mom who saw to it that her children's every need was met. Agnes was as dutiful a wife as she was a mother and household manager. On top of everything else, she was an active volunteer for several civic and charitable organizations. Name the job to be done and you could always count on Agnes.

When Agnes first met Bob at one of the fund-raising events for the food pantry, she was immediately impressed with his amiability and engaging style. And she was really surprised when somebody told her how wealthy and influential he was. He seemed like such a down-to-earth person and his manner was so unassuming. She was equally surprised to learn that he wasn't married. He seemed to be a great catch for anyone. But what was the most surprising were the feelings she found herself having for him.

Agnes never really planned to fall in love. It just happened. And it's not like Bob was making obvious or unseemly advances toward her. It's just that he was always so nice to her. And it's not like he was paying her any special attention. It's just that he seemed to notice her. She was completely bowled over by how much he seemed to appreciate her. She wasn't used to anyone taking so much notice, recognizing her good points, or flattering her in any way.

Agnes's life with her husband, Ben, certainly wasn't a bad one. But it was, without a doubt, just another part of a bland existence. Everyone in her family, from Ben to the kids, seemed to take Agnes for granted. It's not that they overtly demanded very much, but they sure seemed to expect a lot. And Agnes was the kind to give, give, and give. So it really threw her for a loop when Bob showed her so many kindnesses. He never did any big or extravagant things for her, just little things; and he did them often and unprompted. Agnes simply wasn't used to anyone paying her any attention, and it felt really good.

Agnes was as surprised as anyone else about how fast things with Bob seemed to escalate out of control. What began as a harmless little talk over lunch one day became a regular weekly rendezvous at a downtown hotel. And the excitement of it all stood in definite contrast to her normal, boring routine. Agnes was completely swept away.

Agnes didn't come to her senses until Bob had finished using her. At first, their romantic lovemaking was like she'd never experienced before. She thought she simply couldn't live without it and never wanted it to end. But eventually, somehow, it became more like an expectation and a chore. And by the time she realized who Bob really was, how shallow and uncaring he was beneath his charming exterior and the horrible mess she'd made of things, it was almost too late. Ben found out about the affair and their marriage was in big trouble. Fortunately, he didn't simply bolt from the relationship, and he honored her frantic pleas to enter into couples' counseling.

Within a few months of therapy, Agnes came to realize that despite being a fairly decent person overall, she had some significant character flaws. Perhaps the biggest among those flaws was the inordinate need she had for external affirmation and approval. And she would eventually have to admit that it was that particular need that really drove her to participate in all the "giving" activities she had engaged in over the years. Looking back, she was amazed at how much and how often she would bend over backward for the little bit of appreciation that came with seeming so dependable. But Agnes also came to realize that she was never really in the business of giving. Real giving is done freely. What Agnes was really doing most of the time was not so much giving but soliciting—subtly fishing for recognition, attention, and appreciation from others. She had kept a deep secret ever since childhood. Above all else, she wanted to be a princess, receiving the desire and envy of all, even though she inwardly felt like the scrubwoman who deserved no notice and little more than meager wages.

Because Agnes's giving nature was really rooted not in love but rather in desperate need, for most of her life she had found it impossible to believe in an unconditionally loving God. If she had believed in that kind of love and that kind of God, she would have harbored a much different sense of self-worth. Even regarding herself as saved by Christ was not enough to make her feel genuinely valued or appreciate the perfect love of God, who gave us Jesus. Unconditional love and positive regard were not qualities Agnes experienced in her relationship with her authoritarian, demanding, and conditionally approving earthly father. As long as she could remember, she had felt inwardly driven to prove her worth by putting herself completely out for him. If she didn't, she felt nothing from him but distance and rejection. It set her on a course of inordinately putting herself out for others. As a result, she lived most of her life physically, emotionally, and spiritually spent. Outwardly, she appeared gracious, but inwardly, she was desperate. Hungry for something to fill up the void inside her, she had basically lived a life in which she prostituted herself constantly, doing whatever she thought she had to do to secure the appreciation, validation, and affirmation she craved. But underneath it all was an emptiness almost no one could fill, especially Ben. So putting the pieces back together again with him would be no easy task.

Agnes had always needed far more from Ben than any man could reasonably be expected to provide. That's why she sought so much love and approval from so many different sources. And repairing the damage she had done and nurturing a healthier, more intimate relationship with him would be a real challenge. But before she could more honestly and fully commit herself to a deeper relationship with Ben, she would have to become much more aware of and attentive to her own needs. In short, she had to come to understand the sublime wisdom in the Lord's exhortation to love others as we love ourselves—not more than, not less than, but in an equal, and ideally, equally healthy, manner. She would also have to find room in her heart for a God loves who not only unconditionally but also abundantly.

Learning what genuine and healthy self-love is all about and striking the right balance between self-regard and regard for others was difficult for Agnes. I would often encourage her by making an analogy to the instructions flight attendants give passengers on an airplane. When your brain is starving for oxygen, you can't think straight enough to help anyone next to you who might be in distress. That's why it's important to be sure your own oxygen mask is secure first. Then you'll have the presence of mind to know what your neighbor needs and how to possibly help.

Agnes had been gasping not for air but for approval her entire life. This profoundly affected her marriage. She was drawn to Ben because in the beginning he made her feel special. But Ben was not the type to heap abundant, unconditional approval upon her. Agnes not only mistakenly took this as a sign that he was much like her father but also interpreted it as a lack of passionate interest on his part, and it wasn't long before she began yearning for more opportunities to feel loved. Although she was not consciously aware of the fact, getting involved in so many charitable endeavors was a way she could get her "approval fix" without straying into territory that might violate her values. And for his part, Ben was negligent in the approval-giving department because he was completely unaware of the nature and degree of Agnes's need. Their mutual obliviousness prevented them from really knowing each other well enough or relating to each other intimately enough to have a vibrant, passion-filled marriage. In therapy, Agnes and Ben actually got to know each other for the first time.

Agnes came to realize what a good and decent man Ben had always been and how fortunate she was to have him as a life partner. For his part, Ben came to realize how his complacency and tendency to take Agnes for granted invited her to feel underappreciated and undervalued. The more that Ben and Agnes really got to know each other, the more their love for each other deepened. And the more they both witnessed the power of their love to enliven their souls, the more they came to appreciate the love the Lord must have for both of them and how that love might be better manifested in the manner in which they regarded themselves as well as each other. Agnes cut down on some of her outside activities and carved out some time for herself, spending time on the treadmill, doing some reading, and even getting back to the painting she once enjoyed so much. It came as a big surprise to her that as busy as she was, she found herself having not only time left over but also the energy to nurture some quality time with Ben. After almost twenty years of marriage, they were regularly "dating" again! Life was not just becoming good again; it was becoming better than it had ever been.

Christ knows that properly loving ourselves is difficult to do. And this is true for loving someone else as well. You can't really love a person until you first really know him or her. Agnes and Ben came to know themselves and each other at a level they could never have imagined before. Their process of self- and mutual discovery is an ongoing one. So is the process of knowing and loving the Lord. The more intimately you know, the more deeply you can love. This is the timeless truth and lesson Ben and Agnes learned. It strengthened their regard for themselves, their love for each other, and the faith they once professed but now hold more deeply in their hearts.

When Fragile Faith Is Put to the Test

Most of us are fortunate not to be harshly tested. Perhaps we are doubly fortunate on that score because testing reveals not only the defects in our character but also the weakness of our faith. The following story is of a family in which the character of its members appeared intact and everyone's faith appeared strong. Then came the testing, and the cracks became painfully evident.

Mark was Frank and Amy's only son and their pride and joy. He was also a loving older brother to his two sisters. He could always make them laugh and feel protected. Everyone liked Mark. Blessed with good looks and natural charm, he was the guy all of his classmates wanted to be around. And he was quite talented, both intellectually and athletically. He had star power on the football field, on the basketball court, and in the classroom. It was hard to find a soul who had a bad thing to say about Mark, which is what made it so hard to understand the change in him that followed his last military tour of duty.

It was no surprise that Mark wanted to join the army after graduating high school. His parents always believed he had almost as much love for his country as he had for his God and his family. He was openly proud to serve. And he excelled at the academy, graduating in the top ranks of his class. To many in his family and among his circle of friends, Mark was a hero even before he was called into action.

Mark's family didn't really trust their intuition when he returned from his first tour of duty. Something seemed a bit different about him, but it was hard to pinpoint exactly what it was. Sometimes they even thought that they must be imagining things. But by the end of his third and final tour, it was clear that Mark was not the same. He was staying out until all hours, partying with total strangers, using multiple substances throughout the day, coming home wasted, and having major problems finding and keeping work. His girlfriend had already threatened to leave him twice before when she tearfully confided to Mark's parents, to whom she had become very close over the years, that she simply couldn't remain with or consider marrying a person who could call her the horrible names he'd uttered of late. Additionally, he seemed interested only in meaningless sex and had even become physically abusive of her at times.

Mark did not come into therapy on his own initiative, but rather under some fairly persistent pressure from his parents. In such cases, therapy is rarely successful. But in Mark's case, it became clear early on that he had enough internal pain and unhappiness to work with, even though much of it had been repressed. And when all was said and done, it would become apparent that his pain had a lot to do with the loss of faith he had suffered during his deployments. On the surface, Mark had been drowning himself in a sea of drugs, meaningless sexual encounters, and raucous behaviors. But underneath it all, he was severely depressed and doing his best to stave off total despair.

One of the things that became strikingly clear during my work with Mark was that although he had always done the right and noble thing during his early years, he had never claimed personal ownership of the values his parents thought they had instilled in him. He had always thrived on external validation and approval. And early on he adopted the ideals of his parents, teachers, and even his church as the surest means to secure those ends. He never explored or questioned the sentiments of his own heart. Rather, he simply did as others expected and relished the support he received from them in return. As a result, he never made an intimate connection with any of the values to which he'd been exposed yet blindly embraced. He simply couldn't appreciate the wisdom behind those values. And he'd never seriously contemplated or wrestled with the major tenets of his religion. He was an archetypal example of someone with blind faith.

Mark's blanket acceptance in his early years made it almost inevitable that he would fail the many tests of personal faith he would encounter during his stint in active service. During his tours of duty, he saw it all: indiscriminate drug use, callous disregard for life, degradation and rape of women, rampant brutality, abuse of children, and even cold-blooded murder. Worst of all, some of the most horrific acts he witnessed were carried out by people he thought he knew and could trust, many of whom he was once close to and who, like himself, claimed to be believers in God. Once he even witnessed one of his Christian comrades, whom he thought to be his best friend, doing the unthinkable and with apparent pleasure. When Mark went to war, the war waged a full-frontal assault on his tenuous faith.

Soon after the start of his first tour of duty, Mark began to realize that some of his fellow soldiers were there for reasons other than those for which he had initially entered the service. He viewed his enlistment as a way to honor God and country as well as protect his friends and family. He truly came to serve and was proud to do so. And he felt that most of his comrades shared his sentiments. But then he encountered some whom he realized were there primarily for a paycheck and an education they'd find more difficult if not impossible to get anywhere else. He also encountered those who were also looking for a chance to vent tons of pent-up anger and hostility and wield power they hadn't known before by shooting up things, conquering others, and generally wreaking havoc. Slowly, he came to question whether the things he'd once believed in so ardently were actually real. And the various atrocities he witnessed made him wonder if people really cared about anything or anyone except themselves. There was no way for Mark to know whether his experiences were unusual or the norm. It's hard to be objective when you're in the thick of things day in and day out. But as a result of what he had witnessed, Mark eventually came to believe he had been deceived, even by those he once revered. From what he could tell, there was really no such thing as honor or duty. To him, it seemed the facts were clear: there are no heroes. There are only rowdy boys who make sport of unruly behavior and relish the chance to run amok under the pretext of making the world safe.

War had taken a heavy toll on Mark. He not only had to live with the memories of those who had sacrificed life and limb but he also had to carry with him the indelible images that had so deeply pierced his heart and darkened his soul. How could a just and loving God, he questioned, stand so idly by while people starved, captives were savagely beaten and tortured, young girls were raped, and countless lives were ruined? He would eventually have to find his own answers to these and other challenging questions. And he would have to define for himself the principles and ideals that he might one day have the courage to embrace. For most of his life, he had simply accepted what he was told without question and therefore with less than deliberate or genuine conviction. For too long, he believed what he was told he should believe. If he were to really start living again, he would have to take the inordinately difficult and deeply personal leap that defines real faith.

Mark eventually came to discover the value in the principles he had always been taught. He gradually came to that aha moment when he truly understood how inherently flawed human beings are and how essential faith in something quite above ourselves and the ways of the world is to the very salvation of a person's soul. He also came to see quite clearly how his own abandonment of faith had fueled his spiral downward into a life of callous indifference and self-destruction. And only his intimate experience with what life can be like when it's devoid of such a faith could properly equip him to fully appreciate its saving power. He found new and deeper meaning in the values his parents, teachers, and church had always promoted, and which at one time he only parroted. Through his ordeal, Mark became a believer.

Others would eventually begin to view Mark as the person he used to be. And while to these others he appeared to be returning to his former self, Mark would never in fact be either the person he was before he went to war, or the person he became during his experience of war. That's because for the very first time in his life, he was truly becoming his own person, claiming his own core beliefs—beliefs rooted in his own conscious, deliberate, and free leap of faith. So he didn't regain his old self. Rather, he became an entirely new man in faith, a man who not only reckoned with but accepted and repented the many things he and his comrades did that exposed his earlier weakness of faith.

Forgiving himself was not easy for Mark. He'd not only stood by while his comrades committed heartless acts but also engaged in some of these acts himself. But knowing that he had just as freely and willingly laid down his former life as he had embraced a new one eventually allowed him to bestow upon himself a necessary measure of forgiveness for the things he had once done. Mark was happy to shed his former self. It was never a genuine self to start with. And he would never again lead a life of blindly following. Rather, for him it would be an eyes-wide-open existence. And Mark would feel little need to proclaim his newfound faith with words. For the first time in his life he felt he really knew Christ, who he was and what his teachings meant. And he also knew very well what a life can be like lived without him as a guiding influence. Truly accepting Christ as his personal Savior, he would manifest his faith by the life he would deliberately embrace and henceforward lead. The old Mark physically survived the war but almost died in spirit. The new Mark has put the war and his faithless sins behind him and impacts others with his vibrant and infectious spirit.

BELIEFS AND BEHAVIOR

Psychologists and other behavioral scientists have known for some time that there is an inextricable interrelationship between a person's beliefs or attitudes and their behavior. This interrelationship is the basis for the cognitive-behavioral perspective upon which many of the most effective modern therapies are based. How a person thinks about something, the convictions he or she holds, and the attitudes that person harbors will largely determine how he or she will respond in any given situation. Therefore, the advice of a therapist is relatively straightforward: change the way you think about things and you can't help changing the way you act. For example, if a woman believes that an acquaintance did something *to* upset her as opposed to something inadvertently *that* upset her, she will likely respond to the friend in a much different way. Similarly, if a man believes that a woman is meant to be subordinate to him at all times and must be taught to respect his power to keep her from stepping out of line, it should come as no surprise to anyone that he might behave in a domineering, controlling, or perhaps even abusive way with his spouse. What we believe inevitably affects how we act.

How we habitually act also has an effect on our thinking patterns, attitudes, and beliefs. So if you change the way you've habitually been acting, the chances are good that you'll gradually come to see things differently. Changing—even in one's mind-set—is almost always in the doing. Christ understands this interrelationship. That's why he commands us to do the loving thing. He doesn't command us to feel a certain way, or to harbor a certain sentiment. Besides, we don't have all that much control over how we feel anyway. Rather, he commands us to act in a specific manner. Over that, we have greater power. And he knows that it's not just that we will do differently when our hearts and minds are changed. He also knows that our hearts and minds will change (that is, we'll experience *metanoia*), and for the better, as we compel ourselves to do differently, time and time again, from what the world teaches us to do. So once again the path he offers to genuine righteousness and purity of heart is really quite simple: do the loving thing. In fact, as Paul exhorts, we should do everything (1 Corinthians 16:14) with and in love. Doing so will change the way we see, the way we feel, and the way we believe. But once again, as simple as this prescription is, it's definitely not easy.

Professing to others and convincing ourselves on an intellectual level what we believe is one thing, but what we really believe in our hearts is another. A friend once told me that he'd found the most knowledgeable and trustworthy financial advisor he'd ever come across. He insisted the advisor had never been wrong on a stock market prediction and had made millions for all those who had invested with him. I asked my friend if he had therefore turned over all of his holdings to this advisor's management. My friend said that he had invested a portion of his savings with the man but had kept the rest in "conservative and safe" certificates of deposit. I then challenged him about how much faith he actually had in this advisor. His response was, "Oh, I trust him all right. I trust him implicitly. I just trust myself more!"

The heart's true convictions are always revealed not by what we say but by what we do. If Larry, in the story in chapter 1, really had come to believe that his victims were persons of worth, he would never have referred to them as "bitches and whores." If Becky in the story in chapter 4 had really believed that the Lord loved her unconditionally and would provide what she needed, she would never have latched onto Randy just to feel secure, or succumbed to the temptation to take surreptitiously what she feared she couldn't obtain otherwise. And if Martha in the story in chapter 2 had had any faith in God or confidence in the ample gifts given to us all, she wouldn't have made it so easy for her grown son to remain an inadequate child. What we do is the truest reflection of what we believe.

The Apostle James knew well that the most genuine testimony about what one believes is the transformative action his or her faith engenders. He often took issue with Paul, not because Paul was in error to assert that faith is what saves us, but because the manner in which Paul so frequently spoke about this issue might easily convey the impression that an outward, verbal profession of faith is sufficient or is an accurate indication of our true belief. James understood the relationship between true salvation of the spirit and a genuine belief in Christ. And he insisted that faith not evidenced by action is devoid of life and substance. He pointed out that even demons believe in God, yet their faith is not their salvation but rather an additional aspect of their torment. And citing the example of Abraham, whose own faith was both tested and found sound by his willingness to bring his own son to the altar of sacrifice, James dared anyone to prove their faith by anything other than the deeds that manifest it (James 2:16-23). The problem for most of us, including myself, is that as desperately as we want to believe, casting our doubts completely aside and taking the full leap of faith in Christ is a most daunting challenge. And when certain situations present themselves in life and the soundness of our faith and character are tested, our actions bespeak our doubts as well as our shortcomings.

As a Christian and a therapist, I have become convinced of the power of faith and honest self-reckoning to transform people's lives. And I consider it my duty as a helping professional to kindly but firmly challenge those who are in trouble to examine their true beliefs, to be honest with themselves about their intentions, and to make a concerted effort to change both their dysfunctional beliefs and behaviors. It's very different work from traditional insight-oriented psychotherapy. But in our times, most folks need much more than mere insight into their difficulties. Most often, they need to grow and strengthen their character, and growth always entails change. And because real change can only happen in the here and now, they must necessarily be confronted on and demonstrate a willingness to change their distorted thinking or problematic behavior the moment it occurs. So my work has largely become challenging folks to be honest with themselves about themselves, to confront their problematic beliefs and behavior patterns, and to reinforce themselves for daring to think and behave differently. In so doing, they become better persons. But without question, this is an almost insurmountable task in the absence of faith.

CHAPTER 6

FAITH AND THE
HUMAN CONDITION

According to how many interpret the book of Genesis, we are fallen creatures. Despite being fashioned blemish-free by our Creator and initially intended for an immortal existence in an earthly paradise, we turned away from God and are now living with the consequences. Just about all we really had to do, as the story goes, was fulfill the Lord's desire that we multiply and fill the earth. And we were forbidden only one thing: to eat of the fruit of the tree of the knowledge of things good and bad. But as those familiar with the story know all too well, our first parents messed up fairly quickly, doing the very thing they were commanded not to do. As a result, we, their children, experience evil, hardship, and death. To make matters worse, we inherit their original sin, making each one of us flawed from the start. While we are always trying to do it our way in our own time, we only succeed in wandering away from God and toward our desperate need for redemption.

Among the many scientific stances, perspectives on humanity are markedly different. And the dominant framework views humans as ascendant creatures, beginning our existence as cousins of the ape (whose own origins can be traced all the way back to a simple single-celled organism) who evolved steadily over hundreds of thousands of years into the upright-walking, innovative tool–making, and dynamic-thinking creatures we are today. So in the first way of thinking, humans begin as defective creatures, in desperate need of remaking, while the latter way of thinking suggests we are made miraculously and are in a constant state of modification and refinement.

The most profound thing about all the major myths, metaphors, religions, and philosophies is that they all contain kernels of the most powerful and eternal truths, despite the fact that some contain factual inaccuracies and none have the ability to capture the entire, ineffable truth about the ultimate realities. It's simply impossible for us to really know anything with absolute certainty. That's why faith is so essential. I know there is considerable debate among Christian believers about whether the creation myths included in the Bible should be regarded as literal and historical fact. But whether the Eden story is factually accurate is really irrelevant to the larger truth it contains. It's an undeniable reality that none of us is born perfect, and we all fall short of the kind of person we have it within us to be. In that sense, we are indeed fallen creatures, even from birth. And there is also no doubt that we suffer a distinctive anguish that comes with knowing the difference between good and bad and a very real death of spirit that comes with doing bad as often as we do, even while knowing better. But we are also creatures of great promise. And among all of the creatures on this earth, we alone can fully and freely choose to love and serve the Lord of life. Ants dig their tunnels, foxes build their dens, and birds sing their mating rituals along a preordained script, without deviation or decision. They do merely as they were designed and programmed to do. We, on the other hand, as the great creation myth testifies, are distinctly different, capable of following God by choice. And what a difficult choice that is sometimes! It's hard enough to really know what God wants from us, let alone go against our selfish, egocentric inclinations and voluntarily surrender ourselves to God's will.

Despite how hard it is to know and submit to God's will, however, there's some really hopeful and good news. At just the right moment in history, a most unique figure appeared on earth to show us the way. A chosen few heard his words directly, witnessed his actions, and glimpsed his distinctive character. And after seeing the proverbial light and grasping the ultimate reality of who he really was and what he really represented, these special few became forever changed. Armed with a newfound faith in the person they came to regard as the Christ, and infused with the inspiration of the Holy Spirit, they then set out to illuminate the entire world in the hope that all humankind might share "the words of eternal life" (John 6:68).

There are now more than 2.2 billion people who identify themselves as Christians. But being a Christian is more than merely proclaiming oneself to be a follower of Jesus. It's also more than simply affiliating with a particular religious denomination or faith community. And it's far more than verbally testifying to one's acceptance of Christ's role as Savior and Redeemer. To come to a place of genuine faith, every Christian has to honestly and fervently reckon with some fundamental questions:

Just exactly who do you believe the Christ is?

What was his purpose on earth?

What was the intent and meaning of his teachings?

What do his life, his death, and most especially, his resurrection mean?

What does it mean to be a follower of Jesus?

What exactly does it mean to be reborn or remade in spirit?

What does it really mean that faith in Christ saves?

Who Do You Say Jesus Is?

Perhaps nothing is more crucial to one's Christian faith than having a conviction about just who Jesus is. Some among his people thought him an inspired rabbi, preaching noble but impractical and unreachable ideals. Others thought him a blasphemer and heretic, who snubbed and perverted the law and threatened the very survival of the chosen people of God. But others came to believe that he was no ordinary man, and much more than a great prophet. Peter famously declared him the anointed one and son of the living God (Matthew 16:16), imparting to us the "words of eternal life" (John 6:68).

Jesus proclaimed himself to be the very substance of life: sacred bread conferring boundless and eternal existence upon those who made him the source of their spiritual nourishment. Humanity, he noted, comprises body and spirit and simply can't be sustained by earthly bread. Material food provides nourishment only for the body. But God's eternal Word is the food upon which the life of the soul depends (Matthew 4:4). Christ offers himself as the perfect spiritual food, and invites us to take him in and retain him firmly in our hearts (John 6:62-63). Do that, he bids us all, and we'll live boundlessly and eternally. This is an astonishing claim, and one many find hard to truly believe.

Who we believe Christ is really matters. And the strength and character of our faith in him is reflected more accurately by our actions than by what we say we believe about him. While we might confess with our lips that Christ is God incarnate, providing everything we need to access abundant, everlasting life, we often act as one of those in his time on earth who thought him merely a noble but impractical sage who didn't quite understand how the world really works.

Christ's Purpose

How we view Christ's mission and what he came to do for us also matters. And to merely repeat in rote fashion that he came to save us from our sins does not capture the depth of his purpose. Christ himself told us why he had come to us. He came at the Father's behest to be a bright light to the world—a shining, living example of what real, abundant life is all about (John 12:46). His purpose was to draw humankind to him so that those who placed their faith in him might be brought out of the darkness of their earthly perceptions and predispositions and share eternal life. No one has ever seen God, for God is spirit (John 1:18), but in Christ, God's identity and nature are revealed to us. Christ wanted us to know the Father firsthand. He asserted that anyone who really knew him also knew the Father (John 14:8-9), for he was the very essence of the Father made flesh. And he wanted us to truly know ourselves—what our deepest yearnings really are, how we estrange ourselves from the source of life through sin, and how through faith in him we might reestablish communion.

Intent and Meaning of Christ's Teachings

The meaning we ascribe to Christ's life, his words, and his death and resurrection says much about the character of our faith. We don't know that much about his early life, but we know quite a bit about his ministry and teachings. He called those who would be his followers to accompany him on a most uncommon journey into the realm where his father reigns supreme. He described this realm or place of God's reign (Wills, *What Jesus Meant*, 84), which is commonly translated as "the kingdom of heaven" in many different ways and gave us glimpses of it through his various healing works and actions. He also interpreted the Jewish Law and the Prophets in a way that gave them new and enriched meaning and defined true righteousness. And through his ministry he revealed himself to be the living fulfillment of them.

One does not have to contemplate very hard the life and mission of Christ to realize how dedicated he was to our spiritual health and well-being. He did not concern himself with practical matters, politics, or the particulars of religious practice. But he focused like a laser beam on matters of the spirit. Through his ministry, he demonstrated for us the truth of the human condition, the way to access the soul's deepest yearning, and the abundant life that awaits those willing to set aside what the world has taught them and in faith follow him.

Many of Christ's actions and statements were perplexing and provocative, and caused discord among those who bore witness to them. Some of his initial followers, many of whom had left their jobs and even their families to follow him, found what he had to say, especially about creating within themselves a clean heart and suitable place for his dwelling, very hard to hear, let alone accept (John 6:66). They parted company with him and returned to their former lives. But while some of his words and deeds do indeed seem puzzling at first, once you accept the premise that Jesus' sole purpose at every step and turn was to illuminate us on the life of the spirit, things become much clearer. To really understand Christ's earthly ministry, it's critical that we go far beyond knowing all that he did and said. We have to understand what he *meant* by his words and actions (Wills, *What Jesus Meant*, xviii). Those who did grasp the meaning behind his words and deeds eventually came to believe that the person they had come to know intimately must necessarily be the Christ—the anointed one of God and savior of the human race. Peter testified with his lips that he had come to believe this long before the Lord's passion (Matthew 16:16). But the weakness of even Peter's faith and character would be revealed quite clearly when he was tested near the gates of the high priest's courtyard and denied even knowing Jesus (Matthew 26:72). And for many, what Jesus meant by his words and deeds, and the critical importance of that meaning to our spiritual well-being, did not become clear until after his resurrection.

Many of the self-righteous religious leaders of Jesus' time could not embrace him or his teachings because he appeared to place himself above the law on those occasions when he was observed not following its particulars. But Christ asserted he was not at odds with the law, despite his lack of attendance to its details at times. In fact, he advised that "not one letter" of Mosaic law should be stricken or altered until the purpose it served had been completely fulfilled (Matthew 5:18). He even went so far as to claim that anyone tampering with the law would not be regarded very highly in the era when God's reign is finally fully realized (Matthew 5:19). But he also fully understood the intent and purpose of the law and was filled with righteous indignation that so many of the official guardians of their religion and tradition placed such importance on rigorous adherence to its unessential minutiae while simultaneously disregarding or trampling upon its spirit. The specifics of the law (including the rules governing the observance of the Sabbath), he asserted, were crafted for man's benefit (Mark 2:27), and man was not created merely to give blind assent to the law. He explained that Moses knew his people and what they would need in the way of lawful structure to transform themselves from a tribe of slaves into a godly and great nation. Moses therefore fashioned the religious laws as channels for engendering a right spirit in each person. And the value of those laws is only manifested by those who use them to cultivate personal piety. The truly pious don't really have a need for the laws (1 Timothy 1:8). Moreover, any person acting with purity of spirit is necessarily in complete accord with the law, even if he or she fails to observe its every minor detail.

Most of Christ's teaching was about personal piety, purity, and righteousness, and the faith it took to move a person to attain it. His ministry was all about bringing about God's reign on earth. A nation of righteous people is by nature a great nation. And this was the historical yearning of the people to whom he was specifically sent (Matthew 15:25). And he exhorted—yes, even demanded—that the truly righteous among his followers, those who could help bring to reality a more godly kingdom, actually exceed the letter of the law by demonstrating a quality of love consistent with its spirit. That could only be done by a heart pure, clean, and receptive enough to embrace God's presence.

Some observant Jews focused on attaining personal purity by

guarding against defiling themselves with various impurities of the world. But Jesus cautioned that real purity has much less to do with material substances to which we are exposed or might take in, and much more to do with what emanates from us and the intentions in our hearts (Mark 7:15). A pure heart does not hate. A pure heart does not wage war. A pure heart does not condemn or turn a blind eye to the needy, envy, or wish ill toward others. And it is those kinds of things that truly defile us.

Christ heaped his harshest words on those who kept the letter of the law meticulously but treated their brethren with indifference, disdain, or malice. They had totally missed the point of religious observance, he argued. What's worse, despite their "clean" appearing exterior and their self-righteous self-presentation, they were spiritually dead (that is, "whitewashed tombs" [Matthew 23:27]). And it is more than ironic that many of those obsessed with what they might eat found so many of Christ's sayings hard to stomach and demanded signs and wonders from him to testify to his authority to make his claims. They took care to eat only kosher, but found the Living Bread and his teaching unpalatable! It's the disdain, sanctimoniousness, envy, and stubbornness emanating from their hearts that defiled them. And the fact that they demanded proof of Christ's authority as opposed to immediately recognizing the truth of his words and placing their trust in him testified to both the impurity and the hardness of their hearts (Matthew 12:39).

Once, some Pharisees expressed outrage that Jesus would personally extend forgiveness to an individual for his sins. Only God, they argued, could forgive sins. All others simply had to be held to account, especially by the moral authorities. The law simply had to be enforced. But Christ had been widely preaching a message of love and forgiveness, urging that his people forgive their brothers "seventy-seven" times (Matthew 18:22). So for many it came down to who really had the authority and credibility to correctly interpret the meaning, intent, and spirit of the law: the Pharisees or Jesus? To demonstrate his authority as well as expose the spiritual nature of those challenging him, Christ asked what would be an easier feat for a person (that is, require a greater degree of authority or power): to forgive someone their failings, or to make it possible for a completely crippled person to walk again. And when he charged the paralytic to "take [his] mat and walk" (Mark 2:9; John 5:8), Christ proclaimed for the world to witness that:

- as both the Son of Man and the Son of God, he had authority to forgive sins;

- for our own spiritual health, we need to lose our righteous indignation about the sins of others, being ever mindful of our own shortcomings. We can and should forgive one another, and not just occasionally or when it's convenient, but even when it's difficult;

- physical paralysis is a painful enough burden with which humankind must sometimes deal, but rigid adherence to rules as opposed to having a genuine regard for the welfare of humankind for whom those rules were made is a much greater malady and cripples our spiritual development; and

- he can be trusted as having both the authority and the wisdom of knowing exactly what humankind really needs to be whole and *well.*

Christ's miracle with the paralytic was an archetypal example of how he sought to illustrate ultimate spiritual realities with signs and wonders. And this miracle was set in a particular context in which Christ was confronting the shortsightedness of those who were sanctimonious in their self-presentation but not truly righteous in spirit. Christ taught that the body, like the law, can be a vehicle for the propagation of the divine spirit in the world. Physical health is a desirable commodity, no doubt, but what really matters is the salvation and health of the human soul. And Christ demonstrated his understanding and commitment to this priority by healing the paralytic's wounded spirit (through forgiveness) before gracing him with added hope by healing his physical affliction.

No reader of the Gospels can fail to be impressed with how carefully weighed and measured Christ's words and actions were during his ministry. Every healing he performed, every parable he told, and every action he took was mindful and purposeful, carefully designed to convey crucial messages about the human spirit: what its nature is; what it needs to be nourished; and how it must be renewed after being weakened by sin and hardship. Christ took great care to inscribe the meaning of the law and the wisdom of the prophets in our hearts and minds (Jeremiah 31:33; Hebrews 8:10; 10:16).

The Meaning of Christ's Life, Death, and Resurrection

The meaning we ascribe to Christ's death and resurrection is crucial to our faith. As sobering as it is for me to know that Christ died for my sins, it's even more sobering to contemplate why he had to die, and in the manner that was ordained for him.

Knowing our natural skepticism, and our poverty of faith, Christ offered us the ultimate proof that real life comes only by the grace of the Father through the voluntary surrendering of our earthly existence. And he offered us the ultimate sign, "the sign of Jonah" (Matthew 16:4), that we could trust him. If our hearts were pure, we wouldn't need the sign. But in his mercy, God provided us with a sign that by rights should bring anyone to faith.

Christ's level of obedience was the only way any man could redress the sins of Adam and every person since. He was fully human, so he experienced the anguish any of us would experience (Luke 22:42) if called to the baptism to which he was called (Mark 10:28) and subjected to the trial placed upon him. But he remained faithful to the purpose for which he was sent even to the point that he submitted himself to being mocked, tortured, and savagely slain. He freely allowed himself to be hung naked on a tree and branded by earthly authorities as a rightful object of ridicule and pity. And if the drama had ended there, it would have been impressive enough for those who had listened to him, been inspired by him, and followed him to have considered him a great prophet promoting the very best of human ideals. But the drama didn't end there. Christ was raised from the dead triumphantly on the third day. *That* made a much different kind of believer out of some of his followers. This was no ordinary man. He was indeed God incarnate showing us the way to boundless, eternal life! We can safely cast our doubts aside and place our faith in him. God loved us sinners enough to provide us the ultimate sign that could bring even the most doubting among us to faith. And such a faith can save us from all the pitfalls of the flesh, purify our spirits, and make us right with him.

Inspired and energized by their faith, many committed themselves to spread the incredibly good news to as many as would hear it. They passed along the most memorable stories they believed validated their claim, some of which were eventually written down, and all of which were meant to impress upon all seekers of truth and spiritual health that they had indeed found in Christ the way, the truth, and the life, which the Lord himself asserted that he represented. And many were even willing to lay down their lives in witness to this truth. It's a testament to human weakness and lack of faith, however, that some could not bring themselves to faith even after being given the unprecedented sign (Luke 16:31) Christ afforded them (we're even told that one disciple, Thomas, needed to witness the risen Lord in the flesh before he would believe [John 20:25]). How hard it is for any of us to divest ourselves of the ways of the world and to undergo the *metanoia* or change of heart that leads to a rebirth of spirit in faith. Christ knows this well, and he called truly blessed those who had not personally witnessed the sign he offered yet still believed (John 20:29) because only a pure heart could embrace his teachings, as hard as some of them are, in the absence of definitive proof of his authority.

Following Jesus

Jesus himself also told us not only what it really means to be his follower but also what he expects his followers to do. He expects more than merely acknowledging him as Lord and Savior. He does not want us to honor him with our lips while keeping our hearts far from him. He made it clear that accepting him and following his way is about doing the will of the Father, in the manner he so lovingly demonstrated for us (Matthew 7:21). Observing the command he gave us, that we love one another as he loved us (John 13:34), not shouting from the rooftops that Jesus is Lord, is the way he wants us to honor him.

After his ascension, those among his people who accepted his teaching and regarded him as the messiah came to be known as adherents to "the way." This means that Christ's church, from its earliest beginnings, was identified primarily by its constituents' willingness to embrace the model of living Jesus himself exemplified. That willingness arose out of their firm belief that Jesus was indeed the anointed one of God, inaugurating God's reign on earth by instilling God's word and will in the hearts and minds of those open to the way he outlined for us.

But it has always been easy, as the author of Hebrews observed, for those temporally closest to Christ's message, to "drift away" (Hebrews 2:1) from the core of Christian faith. We Christians are the beneficiaries of great institutional vehicles of grace. But our worship rituals, practices, and professions of belief can be quite empty in the absence of an ongoing conversion of our hearts. The core of our faith is that conversion can inspire a new way of living.

Being Born Again

Christians accept that we are all inherently imperfect or sinful creatures. We often miss the mark (another definition of sin) even when we have the best of intentions. But we also believe in the good news that we can be saved from our baser selves and remade of spirit. By repenting our sins and placing our faith in Christ and his eternal word, we can be transformed. We may never be as good as we want, but we can put an end to our self-defeating behaviors through the grace of God and the help and accountability that our community of faith offers. When one takes the leap of real faith, he or she lays down his or her former life. Once reborn, he or she no longer lives but rather Christ lives in him or her (Galatians 2:20). But this level of faith is extremely rare. Most of us live with such doubt that even though we might call ourselves Christian, we continue to live life mostly on the world's terms, acting as our experience has shaped and predisposed us to behave (that is, we talk the talk of the Christian faith but don't walk the walk of a Christ-transformed life). But the kind of faith Christ calls us to is, in fact, the singular vehicle of our salvation. That's why our most fervent prayer ought to be for more faith, which can only come by the grace of God.

Faith That Saves

How does faith in Christ save us? It enables us to lay down our earthly lives and transcend our baser nature. It motivates us to clean our spiritual house and to open a space for his indwelling. The days of the physical temple are past. There is no more need for sacrifice because the perfect sacrifice has already been made. Christ asks us to be God's temple, but we are God's temple together. We were never meant to live out our faith on our own.

Christ asks that we trust and love him enough to keep his words and obey his father's wishes, and he and the father will take up residence in us (John 14:23). Pure vessels of the Spirit don't do the horrible things that plague so much of our daily lives. So why does so much evil still exist in this world of hundreds of millions of "Christians"? Because so many of us don't really live like we say we believe. Faith can indeed save us. If only we had more of it!

What a leap of faith it is to believe that Jesus was more than just another wise sage in the rabbinical tradition, offering a lofty but impractical view of a better world. Most humans respect all such sages as having good intentions and imparting a vision to which we all wish we could aspire but simply can't really embrace. Because although we'd like to believe in such things, in our hearts we know that the world really works in a very different way. To believe that Christ is the incarnate author of life itself with the only valid prescription for living rightly, abundantly, and eternally takes one heck of a leap of faith. But it is precisely that faith that has the power to totally transform each and every one of us, and ultimately, the world. That's what real Christian faith is all about. Believing that Christ is exactly who he said he was: the way, the truth, and the life.

The Perfect Prayer

Jesus shared our nature as well as the Divine nature. So he knows us better than we can possibly know ourselves. He knows how difficult it is for us to have faith. He knows why even the best of us still do bad things. That's why he emphasized in provocative terms what even a small amount of real faith (that is, "faith the size of a mustard seed" [Matthew 17:20]) could do and marveled when he encountered uncommon faith. He knows our weaknesses and vulnerabilities. His perfect understanding of our greatest physical, psychological, and spiritual needs is reflected in the manner in which he taught us to pray.

The paraphrasing of the Lord's Prayer that follows is not primarily intended as either an embellishment or a clarification of Christ's teaching. Rather, it is meant to overcome some of the inherent limitations of language and translation and to demonstrate compatibility with multiple perspectives, paradigms, and principles in a manner that both recognizes and honors Christ's special understanding of the human condition.

All-powerful Spirit and singular creative force behind the universe, may you be revered by every living creature.

May even your ineffable name be held sacred, never called upon or uttered casually, or used for any untoward or self-serving purpose.

May your reign be realized everywhere, and may your will be embraced by all those to whom you have granted the choice to freely love and subordinate themselves unconditionally to you, as is already the case within the realm where you enjoy full dominion.

For ourselves, we humbly ask that you grant us sufficient provisions each day to get us through the next, for we are an anxious and insecure people, prone to abandoning hope and trust during times of want and need, and we are painfully aware that we are more likely to live in the manner you desire for us if we are free of the anxieties of the day.

We ask that we be forgiven our shortcomings and unmet obligations to others just as we strive to accept in love and forgive those whom we perceive have injured or fallen short of their obligations to us.

And knowing our weakness and our proneness to evil under duress or temptation, we ask that we might be mercifully spared those circumstances that put our character and our faith to the test.

We ask these things knowing that ultimately all power, glory, and dominion really belong to you, Lord, now and forever.

That we might truly revere our God, that we know and submit to his will, that we be forgiven our weaknesses, and that we be spared the trials that inevitably test and reveal the deficiencies in our faith and character—these are what the Lord himself prays for us and advises us to pray for ourselves.

The integrity of a bridge cannot be fully or accurately tested unless it's placed under load. Only stress can reveal any structural defects that might eventually bring the structure down. Similarly, our character weaknesses always become more evident during times of testing. The greater or more attractive the temptation we're facing, or the more intense the stress we're under, the more likely our fragile characters are to fracture. Although we are inherently weak and prone to failure, faith in Christ and his eternal Word and participation in a community of faithful believers have the power to strengthen us and save us from many acts of self-destruction. The greater our faith, the more abundant, fulfilled, and secure is the life that awaits us.

Throughout this book I tried to illustrate the most common ways evil enters into people's lives, the character deficiencies that often allow evil to flourish, and the role that faith in Christ and in his Word can play in the amelioration of most human misery. Much of what I asserted through the vignettes was intended to be provocative. It's my sincerest desire to challenge you, as I challenge myself daily, to make our Christian faith more than the label by which we identify ourselves and to embrace that faith as a dynamic, ever-present motivator for a new life in Christ, who came to save us all.

AN EVER-EVOLVING LIFE OF FAITH AND CHARACTER GROWTH

I 've dedicated much of my professional career to helping folks heal from debilitating psychological, emotional, and spiritual pain. And while some of that pain came about as the result of truly unpredictable and tragic occurrences, more often the pain I witnessed stemmed primarily from the deficiencies in people's character exposed when they were tested by trying circumstances that they could not overcome because of the poverty of their faith. That made the task of providing appropriate counsel one of encouraging them not only to honestly reckon with their personal shortcomings but also to more seriously contemplate the nature of their core beliefs.

Over the years, I have dealt with a lot of suffering. And some of it has definitely been what I will term "destructive." By "destructive," I mean pain that appears to serve no purpose other than to wound or devastate a person's spirit. Pain can be destructive for several reasons. Sometimes, pain enters a person's life with such intensity or in such a traumatic manner that it overwhelms even the healthiest individual's capacity to cope. Other times, a person lacks the emotional, psychological, or spiritual resources to deal effectively with the pain. Usually, destructive pain results from a combination of these factors. And when such pain occurs, it can have a crushing and detrimental impact on a person's mental, emotional, and spiritual well-being. I have also witnessed suffering that many have called "constructive," because it proved instrumental in helping a person learn and grow. And when pain is constructive, it doesn't seem to matter how intensely we hurt as much as how we bear and deal with our suffering. But there is one thing I have come to believe makes the difference between whether suffering is ultimately destructive or constructive, and that is faith.

There's no greater test of the nature and strength of our faith than suffering. Suffering tests our faith as well as our character. And as the Apostle James noted many years ago, when faith is tested, it can even be an opportunity for joy because holding to one's faith in the midst of suffering builds some vital virtues into one's character (James 1:2-3). I've witnessed people working through all sorts of suffering whose steadfast, reclaimed, or newfound faith enabled them to become renewed in spirit as well as strengthened in character.

Despite our shortcomings and failings, we are all called to discipleship. Jesus personally called both Peter and Judas. And because both were looking for something, they heeded the call. Each would face their own tests of character and faith. And while

Peter, despite his earlier boasts, denied Jesus when placed under duress, he repented. Peter, forgiven and strengthened in faith by the Lord's resurrection, went on to do great things and to be the "rock" of the faith he was called to be. Judas, on the other hand, could not overcome his wounded pride and the pain associated with his exposure. Judas ended his own life. The most tragic aspect of the *Judas Syndrome* is that when we completely abandon our faith, we can succumb to despair.

It's humbling for me to testify about the saving power of faith, knowing how lacking I am in it. It's even more humbling to talk about the power of faith in Christ and the power of that faith to heal and renew a person's spirit (several examples of which I have included in this book) because even though I witnessed it first-hand and should be among the most fervent of believers, I know my faith is still weak. So in a very real way, this book is much more of a confession than it is a testimony.

Not only am I weak in faith but I also have my own deficiencies of character, which I struggle daily to overcome. And there have been many times in my life, some of which were quite serious, when my character was put to the test and was found woefully lacking. So my purpose in writing this book is not to preach to anyone my perfect understanding of either faith or the human condition, but to share my experience, and in so doing to testify to the truths I have come to learn. I hoped to inspire greater faith in those finding value in the insights and experiences I sought to share, and in the process I found an avenue to reinforce and solidify my own sometimes feeble faith. And because faith is ultimately one of the three virtues that only God can confer upon us, my most frequent and fervent prayer is for greater faith.

I am a Christian by faith and a psychologist by training. I am also an ardent seeker of the truth. But truth is often elusive. And because the ultimate truths are so incomprehensible, we have always had to rely on various metaphors (religious, scientific, philosophical, and psychological, etc.) to help us grasp them. I have always strived to reconcile the different metaphors. And there have been many others within the psychological community (Carl Jung being the most notable example) who have strived to find harmony among psychological precepts, philosophical principles, and religious beliefs and practices. Truth is truth, no matter what metaphor it derives from, and no single metaphor has a corner on the truth. And for any particular metaphor to rightly lay claim to any truth, it must be able to reconcile its perspective with the truths emanating from other metaphors. Many times, especially when it comes to the bigger truths, we end up saying the same thing but in different ways with each metaphor, each perspective containing an essential kernel of the truth but no single viewpoint capable of adequately conveying the whole truth. And sometimes we take our metaphors much too seriously. It would be foolish to think we could capture the essence of being human beings by making a list of the organic compounds that compose one's body (as one scientific metaphor would postulate). All metaphors contribute something. But we move far away from the truth when we become narrowly immersed in any one of them. Even religious viewpoints can be adopted so rigidly and narrow-mindedly that we lose sight of the bigger truth.

As I have written earlier (*Character Disturbance*, 14), I believe that we have been living in an age of fairly rampant character disturbance for some time now. But I have also come to fervently believe that we are on the cusp of a new age, and that some of our most long-enduring metaphors will have to give way to new and more accurate ways of discerning the important truths about the world in which we live. We face a monumental challenge and a daunting new frontier, and it does not concern the conquest of space or time or solving the mysteries of subatomic matter. The real final frontier is *us*. And that's because if we don't succeed in becoming fully honest with ourselves about ourselves, and with one another about one another, we're probably not going anywhere. We already know too much and there are too many disturbed characters among us. The right amount of plutonium in the wrong hands could easily spell unimaginable disaster. And although I believe that many of our philosophical, scientific, psychological, and even religious metaphors have ceased serving us well, our need for Christ and his message could not possibly be greater. Perhaps the new myth we need to guide us and that more fully embraces Christ's message is just around the corner. I know in my heart how badly we need it and I must believe it is coming.

The main thing I've tried to share with you in this book is my conviction that what we believe makes a difference in how we do things, and conversely, that doing things differently can change our beliefs. Christ came to tell and show us how to live—really *live*. Not in fear of death, not in anxiety about tomorrow, not in competition with or in judgment of one another, but in complete and total love of and confidence in God and our surrendering to God's will. While our bodies struggle for power and lust after material possessions to survive and prosper, our souls yearn only for communion with the divine. We have a choice: we can either succumb to living on the animal plane (that is, the "world's" terms), or in faith surrender ourselves to God and access eternal life in communion with God. Christ showed us God's face. He showed us what we're destined for if we heed the call. He even told us how to cultivate the clean heart necessary to make a space for his residence within us. But just as Adam and Eve freely chose to turn away from God, we can only turn back to God of our own free accord. We are by nature deeply conflicted, a house divided against ourselves (Matthew 12:25). Our souls want to leap but our flesh wants to hang on to what's brought us pleasure and enabled us to avoid pain. We desperately need encouragement. We need a reason for faith in something more. By his very life, and most especially by his death and resurrection, Christ gave us the perfect cause to believe. He is the best possible reason God could give us for hope. If we can bring ourselves to really trust in him, to take the leap, we can be rescued from the trap we've made for ourselves within. Faith in Christ can indeed save us. But we have to take the leap. And if we really do it, our lives simply can't be the same again. There is no need to preach it, for our faith should be self-evident to the world.

Here for me, in a nutshell, is what it means to be the fallen creature I am: I know in my heart that what I have said is true. I have witnessed too much of the Spirit's workings to deny it. And I desperately want to take that leap. But I also know that I still struggle with fears and doubts, and lack sufficient faith to fully do so. Pray for me, as I will pray for you.

REFERENCES

Alcoholics Anonymous. *Twelve Steps and Twelve Traditions.* Chicago: Alcoholics Anonymous World Services, 2002.

Emmons, Robert A. *Thanks! How the Psychology of Gratitude Can Make You Happier.* New York: Houghton Mifflin Harcourt, 2007.

Emmons, Robert A., and Michael E. McCullough. *The Psychology of Gratitude.* New York: Oxford University Press, 2004.

Peck, M. Scott. *The Road Less Traveled.* New York: Touchstone, 2003.

Rohr, Richard. *The Naked Now.* New York: Crossroad, 2009.

Ruiz, Don Miguel. *The Mastery of Love.* Sonoma: Amber Allen Publishing, 2002.

Sanford, John. *Mystical Christianity.* New York: Crossroad, 1993.

Sanford, John A. *The Kingdom Within.* New York: Harper Collins, 1987.

Simon, George. *Character Disturbance: The Phenomenon of Our Age.* Little Rock: Parkhurst Brothers, 2011.

———. *In Sheep's Clothing: Understanding and Dealing with Manipulative People.* Little Rock: Parkhurst Brothers, 2010.

Wills, Garry. *What Jesus Meant.* New York: Viking, 2006.

Zweig, Connie, and Jeremiah Abrams, eds. *Meeting the Shadow.* New York: Penguin, 1991.